Business Resources
on the Internet

A Hands-On Workshop

Internet Workshop Series Number 3

Supplement to
Crossing the Internet Threshold

Gary R. Peete

Library Solutions Press
Berkeley and San Carlos, California

First edition: April 1995
Second printing: January 1996 Minor revisions

Graphics Editors: Catherine Dinnean and Stephanie Lipow

Copyright © 1995 Gary R. Peete

LIBRARY SOLUTIONS PRESS

Sales Office: 1100 Industrial Road, Suite 9
                       San Carlos, CA 94070

Fax orders: 415-594-0411

Telephone orders: 415-592-8904

Web URL: http://www.library-solutions.com

Email: info@library-solutions.com
                       [Leave the subject and message blocks blank; you will
                       receive an automated response.]

Editorial Office: 2137 Oregon Street, Berkeley, CA 94705

ISBN: 1-882208-10-2

Table of Contents

Foreword by Anne G. Lipow v

Preface ix

Ready Reference Guides

    Best Bets for Exploration: Pre-Workshop Exercise 3

    Glossary 18

    Quick Guide to Telnet, FTP, and Gopher Commands 20

    Background Reading: A Bibliography 22

BUSINESS RESOURCES ON THE INTERNET: THE WORKSHOP

    Before You Start the Workshop 23

    Overview of a Moving Target 24

Module 1: Introducing the Internet 27

    What is the Internet?

    Trends and developments

    Number of commercial networks

    Commercial use

    How to get access

    What you can do

    Network addresses

    Uniform Resource Locators (URLs)

    Those frustrating moments

Module 2: Email 39

    Uses of email

    How to read email addresses

    Finding an email address

    Discussion groups

    How to join a listserv

    Exercise: Join a business discussion group

Module 3: Telnet 47

   Basic Facts about Telnet

   Telnet commands

   Using Telnet to access business information via
      the Library of Congress

   Using Telnet to access legal resources

Module 4: FTP 67

   Basic facts about FTP

   FTP commands

   Using FTP to retrieve software (Mosaic)

   Using Archie to locate information by subject

Module 5: Gopher 83

   Basic facts about Gophers

   Gopher commands

   Bookmark commands

   Finding business-related statistics:

       research resources

       economic indicators and data

       economic bulletin board

       current business statistics

       labor force, employment, and earnings data

   Using Veronica to find the Consumer Price Index

Module 6: World Wide Web 109

   Problems and promises

   Using Mosaic to find:

       markets and investment information

       corporate reports

       quarterly earnings reports

       10-K reports

   Tips for customizing your Web browser
      for speed or ease

Index 133

Foreword by Anne G. Lipow, Series Coordinator

About This Series...

At Library Solutions Institute, which offers Internet training programs worldwide, we haven't figured out how to clone our experienced trainers, so we've taken their workshops and put them into book form. The volumes of the Internet Workshop Series are the authors' actual workshops: their well-tested lectures, demonstrations, exercises, and handouts. The series is, therefore, intended to be useful to two types of reader: the learner and the trainer.

Each title comes in two editions: the "book-alone" edition and the "PLUS" edition. With one exception, the book-alone edition is intended primarily for the learner. That exception is Vol. 1, *Introducing the Internet*: both versions of the book are intended for the trainer who is preparing an introductory lecture and demonstration (not a hands-on session). The book-alone editions are also useful to trainers as models on which to pattern their own, and some of the titles include the presentation slides in full-size form from which the trainer can make transparencies.

The PLUS edition is intended specifically for the trainer and always includes the presentation slides—in full-size for making transparencies, as well as on disks (Macintosh and Windows) for displaying the slides from a computer. If the owner has the PowerPoint software, the slides can be customized.

For the learner, each title is a self-paced workshop-in-a-book. We have carefully designed the pages, including the exercises, to compensate for the missing live instructor. However, one critical piece of the live workshop is missing: the class discussion. So to experience, though in a delayed fashion, the give-and-take between instructor and student, we urge you to note your questions in the margins and email them to the instructors. (Their email addresses can usually be found at the end of a section in the Preface.) Future printings may be revised to answer such questions for later readers.

For the trainer, each volume provides a model training tool. With the astounding rate of growth of the Internet, it is likely that as soon you learn about an aspect of the Internet, you'll be asked to explain it to others. Of course, knowing a subject is one thing; teaching it so that your audience learns is quite another. That's the primary reason for the PLUS editions: by example to provide the new trainer with the basic skills needed for a successful instructional program. Each volume gives you the words and supporting materials of a proven training session and provides asides to the trainer: for example, advice about how to handle a tricky segment; the principle underlying a particular way of dealing with a topic; the equipment needed for the session. PLUS edition purchasers are welcome to use the lecture and overheads for their own in-person instructional sessions only. Trainers may wish to coordinate bulk orders of the book-alone edition for use as a student workbook, available at a discount from the publisher. For questions about bulk orders or for clarification of copyright issues, please contact us at sales@library-solutions.com.

Whether you are a learner or a trainer, your comments about the usefulness of the volume you are using are most welcome. Please address them to the author, whose email address can be found in the Preface to each book.

and this book...

If you are looking for a good hands-on workshop on how to find business resources on the Internet, this is it. You could either come to Berkeley and take Gary Peete's popular class, which he gives to a variety of constituencies in and outside of the University of California, or you could sit in the privacy of your office or home and take the workshop by going through this book. Either way, you'll get step-by-step guidance in using the variety of Internet tools to find a wide range of information sources needed by business practitioners, educators, and researchers.

Gary has managed to take the vastness of the Internet in all its complexities and bring it down to size. So if you have felt overwhelmed at the mere thought of setting out onto the "superhighway," you will appreciate the ease with which you are able to "visit" faraway sites and retrieve answers to your business-related questions.

What you are not getting from this "workshop-in-a-book" that you would get from sitting in Gary's class is his clear, patient, calming voice that gives his students a special confidence that this material is really quite logical and easy to grasp, and a personal speaking style that encourages his students to ask questions. You'll have to imagine the voice, but to ask him a question, just drop Gary a note: gpeete@library.berkeley.edu. He's good about answering.

You will notice that Gary's lecture-with-overheads walks you through each lesson by showing what you actually see on the screen each step of the way. In preparation for his live sessions, Gary rechecks each of the sites and services he takes you to and invariably finds that something about them has changed. Some resources at a site disappear from one day to the next without warning; some service that was offered suddenly is dropped; addresses change. Though the resources

BONUS!
As of this printing, you can keep abreast of URLs and services cited in "Best Bets for Exploration" by visiting the author's Web homepage:

http://
www.lib.berkeley.edu
/autobiography
/gpeete/

Gary introduces you to in this book were chosen for their relative reliability of presence, you should not be surprised if, as you try to follow along on your own computer, a screen looks different, or a menu has different offerings, or an address you try doesn't work. (See sidebar on the previous page for how to keep up with changed addresses.)

Before you begin the workshop itself, I urge you to do the pre-workshop exercise (beginning on page 3): "Best Bets for Exploration." It will not only give you a sense at the outset of the incredible breadth of information you can find on the Internet but will also serve to customize the workshop to fit your personal interests. You will flag entries (services, sites, topical discussion groups) you want to explore on your own, which in turn will dictate which module(s) you'll want to concentrate on most or first.

If you are a trainer looking for a ready-made session, complete with lecture, slides, demonstration scripts, exercises, and handouts, this again is what you are looking for. The diskettes, which come with the PLUS edition of the book, contain the slides, which were created in PowerPoint.

Using the Viewer file, you do not need to own PowerPoint to display the slides. If you do own the software, you can edit the slides to suit your own presentation.

About the Author

Gary Peete has spent more than 20 years as an information specialist and teacher. During this time at the University of California, Santa Barbara, and later at the University of California, Berkeley, he has been active in planning and developing various electronic information systems. In recent years, he helped design and establish a local area network of CD-ROM-based information within the UC Berkeley library system and mount the 1990 Census of Population and Housing on an Internet-accessible platform at the Lawrence Berkeley Laboratories.

Gary has taught numerous courses in research methodology in the social sciences and business. While at UC Santa Barbara, he was an instructor in the political science department and taught legal and tax research. He also taught a course on government documents for the Library and Information School at the University of Southern California. Gary has been a frequent guest lecturer in the UC Berkeley School of Information Management Systems. In addition to his offerings to students and faculty in an academic environment, Gary has provided instruction and given workshops to the general public on such topics as legal research, genealogy, government information policy, and electronic information access issues. He currently conducts classes for the Haas School of Business students in using research tools such as Dow Jones News Retrieval System, LEXIS/NEXIS, and the Internet.

At state and national library association conferences, Gary has given presentations on IRS-produced information, researching the Pacific Rim market, locating legislative information, setting up CD-ROM workstations, converting card catalogs to electronic format, tax research, and the consolidation of reference services.

Among the awards and honors Gary has received are election to Phi Beta Kappa, Phi Kappa Phi, and Beta Phi Mu. He has also received many grants and scholarships, including an NDEA fellowship, UC Instructional Development grants, and a California State scholarship.

Gary is head of reference services at the Thomas J. Long Business & Economics Library, University of California, Berkeley.

Preface

As a graduate student studying library and information science in the early 1970s, I became fascinated with the potential of the computer as a tool for storing and disseminating information. At that time, I realized that the computer was a rather restricted tool with limited availability—primarily for those people who had mainframe access and the extensive training that was required to use it. I watched with equal fascination over the ensuing two decades as this once-exclusive instrument became increasingly more accessible to the general population. The introduction and evolution of the personal computer, the development of menu- and graphics-based software, and the ability to connect PCs to high-speed communication networks transformed this once-restricted device into a relatively egalitarian means of storing, finding, transmitting, and manipulating information.

During this continual transformation, I have tried to keep abreast of this rapidly evolving world and integrate electronic material into the offerings available to our clientele, who range from university students and faculty to corporation personnel and small-business owners. With the opening up to the general public of the Internet and its ability to communicate almost instantly with computers anywhere in the world, I saw a tremendous need to keep information seekers, with their diverse interests, aware of all the new options that they have and to show them the business applications of the Internet. In response to this need, I developed various classes that help them make the leap, as painlessly as possible, from the paper environment of the past to the electronic environment of the future.

The lectures I developed for this purpose were designed to introduce this clientele to Internet basics and provide a foundation for later exploration and self-learning. This book will hopefully provide the reader with the same basis for growth and encourage those interested in the Internet to explore the business-related frontiers of this new and ever-changing electronic world.

From my own experiences and those of my students, I would also throw out a word of caution. Any time you are dealing with computers, particularly ones that are networked, prepare yourself for some frustrating experiences. Murphy's Law might well have been written with computer users in mind: whatever can go wrong will go wrong. But don't be discouraged. Pick yourself off the mat, dust yourself off, and start over again. Setbacks are part of the total experience.

Acknowledgements

I would like to thank my wife, Cindy, for her continual support, encouragement, and wise counsel. Also, I'm grateful to the staff at Library Solutions—Anne Lipow, Charlotte Bagby, and Catherine Dinnean—for sharing their splendid suggestions and editorial assistance.

gpeete@library.berkeley.edu
April 1995

Ready Reference Guides

Best Bets for Exploration: Pre-Workshop Exercise

Glossary

Quick Guide to Telnet, FTP, and Gopher Commands

Background Reading: A Bibliography

Best Bets for Exploration: Guide To Internet Resources

Please visit my homepage from time to time to update these best bets:

http:// www.lib.berkeley.edu /autobiography/ gpeete/

This guide provides primary Internet locations for exploring business-related information and sites that will keep you up to date. It is neither exhaustive nor definitive. The evolving nature of the Net would make any such claim frivolous. The sites that have been included in this directory have been selected for their stability and general utility.

However, appearance in this guide is no guarantee that when you go to access any particular database, it will be available. Resources on the Internet are at best mercurial. If you fail to make the desired connection on your first attempt, retry at a future time when the database may be available.

The sites are arranged by broad subject categories. Each entry provides the following information:
- Name of the site, database, or service
- A brief annotation
- Uniform Resource Locator (URL) and email addresses
  Gopher, World Wide Web, Telnet, FTP, or email addresses are provided as appropriate to the type of information being accessed.

For instructions on how to subscribe to the items that are described as listserv lists, discussion groups, or newsletters, see Module 2, Email, page 45. Directions for obtaining information from other email addresses are included in the citations.

The subject categories are as follows:
- General Information
- Accounting
- Economic Information
- Entrepreneurship
- Finance and Investment
- Foreign Business and International Trade
- Government Publications and Legal Resources
- Management
- Marketing Information
- Operations and Statistical Methods
- Personnel, Human Resources

For a few good references to printed sources on how to use the Internet as well as to recent publications on the business use of the Internet, see the section *Background Reading: A Bibliography,* page 22.

SPECIAL INSTRUCTIONS

 Start the workshop by checking off the Internet sites and resources in this list that interest you. Then, after going through each module, refer to this list for sites to practice on and explore.

Best Bets: General Information

☐ **ACADEMIC LISTSERVS**

To obtain a list of listservs in business and economics, email to the address below, leaving the subject line blank.

Email listserv@kentvm.kent.edu

In the body of the message, type: get acadlist file7

☐ **BABSON COLLEGE**

This Gopher site is a good example of a well-rounded and well-arranged Internet information source. It provides easy access to a number of business-related topics and resources, including the COLIS online case study index.

Gopher gopher.babson.edu:70

☐ **BUSINESS SOURCES ON THE NET: BSN 2nd Edition**

This guide provides citations to a large number of sources and is arranged by business subject.

FTP ksuvxa.kent.edu (Files are located in "library directory.")

Gopher refmac.kent.edu/

☐ **BUSLIB-L**

This library discussion group helps keep information specialists up to date on business-related issues.

Email listserv@idbsu.bitnet

listserv@idbsu.idbsu.edu

☐ **CICA WINDOWS ARCHIVE** (Indiana University)

Indiana University provides free access to many software programs that are used to update Windows and search the Internet, including updated versions of Mosaic.

FTP ftp.cica.indiana.edu/pub/pc/win3

Web http://www.cica.indiana.edu

☐ **COMMERCENET**

This Web site is an advertising and commercial consortium operated by Enterprise Integration Technologies and demonstrates how parts of the Net have evolved into a for-profit enterprise.

Web   http://www.commerce.net

☐ **COMMERCIAL SERVICES ON THE NET**

This Web site is a current source for locating products and services advertised on the Net and for use on the Net.

Web   http://www.directory.net

☐ **THE GATE: FROM THE SAN FRANCISCO CHRONICLE AND SAN FRANCISCO EXAMINER**

The Gate provides the full text of most articles in these two newspapers and contains both the current day's news as well as older editions.

Web   http://www.sfgate.com/

☐ **GOPHER JEWELS**

Jewels provides timely information on new Gopher servers.

Gopher   cwis.usc.edu:70/

☐ **INKTOMI SEARCH ENGINE**

This is a new and very fast search software for locating specific information on the Internet.

Web   http://inktomi.berkeley.edu/

☐ **LONG BUSINESS & ECONOMICS LIBRARY, U.C. BERKELEY**

This homepage contains information about the library and the full text of a number of valuable business research guides in the *Berkeley Business Guides* directory. These research guides list the best sources, both paper and electronic, on topics such as companies, investment, foreign markets, statistical sources, and taxation.

Web   http://library.berkeley.edu:80/BUSI/

☐ **NETSURF**

This newsletter is a fun and informative source of information for new developments on all aspects of the Internet, including new business-related sites.

To join, type: subscribe ns-digest-ascii *Yourfirstname Yourlastname*
              or subscribe ns-digest-www *Yourfirstname Yourlastname*

Email   beta@netsurf.com

☐ **RICEINFO**

This Gopher server gives subject access to a number of business-related Gopher servers.

Gopher   riceinfo.rice.edu:70/

☐ **YAHOO** (Stanford University)

Stanford University's Web index is an excellent gateway to resources on all topics, including business and economics.

Web   http://www.yahoo.com/

Best Bets: Accounting

☐ **ANET: THE INTERNATIONAL ACCOUNTING NETWORK**

This site covers many topics on accounting, including

- auditing
- ethics
- financial accounting
- history
- new works
- teaching

Email   Anet-Adm@scu.edu.au
Gopher   anet.scu.edu.au
Web   http://anet.scu.edu.au/ANetHomePage.html

☐ **CTI-ACC-AUDIT@MAILBASE.AC.UK**

A discussion group for those interested in auditing and who desire contact with others with similar interests.

To subscribe, email to:

mailbase@mailbase.ac.uk
In message block, type:
join cti-acc-business *Yourfirstname Yourlastname*

☐ **CTI-ACC-BUSINESS@MAILBASE.AC.UK65**

A discussion group for those interested in using computers for teaching accounting and finance.

To subscribe, email to:

mailbase@mailbase.ac.uk
In message block, type:
join cti-acc-business *Yourfirstname Yourlastname*

EDGAR82

EDGAR provides access to recent electronic filings to the Securities and Exchange Commission.

Email   mail@town.hall.org

        Type "help" in the body of the message to obtain instructions on how to use the email service.

FTP   town.hall.org/edgar

Gopher   town.hall.org

Web   http://www.town.hall.org/edgar/edgar.html

FEDTAX-L@SHSU.EDU (Sam Houston State University)

Sam Houston State University's unmoderated discussion source on trends in federal taxation.

Email   listserv@shsu.edu

Best Bets: Economic Information

CORRYFEE

A discussion group for those interested in economic issues and developments.

Email   listserv@hasara11.bitnet

ECONDATA

A source for national and regional economic data located at the University of Maryland.

Gopher   gopher.inform.umd.edu:70/11/EdRes/Topic/Economics/EconData

ECONOMIC BULLETIN BOARD

One of the primary sources for statistical information on the economy of the United States. It is up to date and contains many historical files.

Gopher   gopher://una.hh.lib.umich.edu

ECONOMIC WORKING PAPERS

A good site for locating and retrieving recent working papers in economics and management.

Gopher   wuecon.wustl.edu

☐ **FDIC DIRECTORY**

Federal Depository Insurance Corporation provides banking and consumer information, bibliographies, and statistics.

FTP   fdic.sura.net

Gopher   nic.sura.net/   (ftp gateway to ftp.sura.net)

☐ **NATIONAL TRADE DATA BANK**

An online version of information from the National Trade Data Bank (NTDB), this site provides economic information on most countries.

Web   http://www.doc.gov/cgi-bin/enter_query/public/sample

☐ **RELOCATION SALARY CALCULATOR**

This Web site calculates the relative cost of living for hundreds of U.S. cities.

Web   http://www.homefair.com/homefair/cmr/salcalc.html

☐ **TIME SERIES DATA**

This FTP site at the U.S. Bureau of Labor Statistics has long runs of national account and labor data.

FTP   stats.bls.gov/pub/time.series/

Web   http://stats.bls.gov/blsome.html

Best Bets: Entrepreneurship

☐ **BIG DREAMS**

This Canadian publication is a monthly newsletter devoted to personal development and topics related to starting a small business.

Web   http://www.wimsey.com/~duncans/

☐ **BUSINESS RESOURCE CENTER**

The Khera Communications' Business Resource Center (formerly Small Business Help Center) is designed to assist businesses obtain information to help them grow.

Web   http://www.kcilink.com/brc/

☐ **ENTREPRENEURSHIP GOPHER** (EGOPHER) (St. Louis University)

Egopher provides a comprehensive gateway to information on starting and operating a business.

Gopher   gopher://sluava.slu.edu:70/11gopher%24root%3A%5Bdata
                     21._general._entrepreneurship%5D

ENTREPRENEURS ON THE WEB

This Web site has two major departments: business information resources and goods and services.

Web http://sashimi.wwa.com/~notime/eotw/EOTW.html

ESBDC-L

This unedited discussion group is interested in Small Business Development Centers.

Email listser@lst01.ferris.edu

NEWPROD

This unmoderated list focuses on the new product development process. Subscription information is available via email.

Email majordomo@world.std.com

SMALL BUSINESS ADVANCEMENT NATIONAL CENTER

This Center is a national and international research, training, consulting, and information center funded primarily by the U.S. Congress and administered by the U.S. Small Business Administration. It contains the largest electronic library in the world pertaining to small business and entrepreneurship.

FTP 161.31.2.174
Gopher 161.31.2.174
Web http://161.31.2.174/

Best Bets: Finance and Investment

ECONDATA (University of Maryland)

EconData provides various financial data tables found in the blue pages of the *Survey of Current Business.*

FTP inform.umd.edu:/info/EconData
Gopher inform.umd.edu
Telnet inform.umd.edu (login as "gopher")
Web http://www.inform.umd.edu:8080/Educational_Resources /AcademicResourcesByTopic/EconomicsResources/EconData /.www/econdata.html

☐ **EDGAR**

EDGAR allows access to electronic filings submitted to the
Securities and Exchange Commission.

Email   mail@town.hall.org
>   Type "help" in the body of the message to obtain instructions
>   on how to use the email service.

FTP   town.hall.org/edgar
Gopher   town.hall.org
Web   http://www.town.hall.org/government databases/SEC EDGAR Documents

☐ **EDGAR CIK AND TICKER LOOKUP**

A Web site that searches the EDGAR database and reveals whether a company
files reports electronically with the Securities and Exchange Commission.

Web   http://edgar.stern.nyu.edu/cik.html

☐ **EMAIL QUOTER**

This site contains various stock-related information, including selected daily prices.

Email   Martin.wong@sun.com
FTP   dg-rtp.dg.com/pub/misc.invest/quote-dump

☐ **FEDERAL DEPOSIT INSURANCE CORPORATION**

The FDIC provides both historical and current banking statistics.

Gopher   gopher.sura.net

☐ **FEDERAL RESERVE BOARD DATA**

This site features large amounts of statistical data on the banking industry,
including interest rates, assets and liabilities, and reserves.

FTP   town.hall.org
Gopher   town.hall.org:70/11/other/fed
Web   http://www.town.hall.org

☐ **FINANCIAL ECONOMICS NETWORK** (FEN)

FEN has various discussion groups available for the scholar interested in
commercial and investment banking, government policies, and companies.
There are 25 channels that break down the topic of financial economics into
subtopics such as banking and corporate finance. To join this group, request
a subscription from Professor Wayne Marr of Clemson University or
Professor John Trimble of Washington State University.

Email   marrm@clemson.clemson.edu *or* trimble@vancouver.wsu.edu.

FINWEB — A FINANCIAL ECONOMICS WWW SERVER

The primary objective of FINWeb is to list and link to Internet resources providing substantive information concerning economics and finance-related topics.

Web http://www.finweb.com/

HOLT'S STOCK MARKET REPORTS

Holt's reports provide daily information on stock markets and commodities, including indexes and prices.

Gopher wuecon.wustl.edu:671/11/holt

HOOVER'S ONLINE

Hoover's Online contains both free and for-fee information on companies. The fee-based service mirrors the information found in the printed Hoover's handbook series.

Web http://www.hoovers.com/search/srch2.cgi

INSTITUTE OF BUSINESS AND ECONOMIC RESEARCH (IBER)

(University of California, Berkeley)

This Gopher site provides citations to a working papers series on finance, 1990–present.

Gopher uclink.berkeley.edu:1605/1

INTERNAL REVENUE SERVICE HOMEPAGE

This IRS Web site contains fileable tax forms, instructions, and answers to frequently asked questions.

Web http://www.ustreas.gov/treasury/bureaus/irs/irs.html

MONEY & INVESTING UPDATE FROM THE WALL STREET JOURNAL

Money & Investing provides free, full-text articles from current Dow Jones publications.

Web http://update.wsj.com

NBER Working Papers (National Bureau of Economic Research, Harvard University)

This index to working papers includes banking and finance. Coverage is from 1978–present and is updated weekly.

Gopher nber.harvard.edu/

NetEc

This electronic collection of working papers produced by universities and research institutions contains finance-related information from 1988 onward.

Web http://netec.wustl.edu/NetEc.html

☐ **PAWWS FINANCIAL NETWORK**

PAWWS provides current quotes, historical graphs, brokerage services, automatic stock tracking, and other investment information and services. Some services are free, while others are fee based.

Web   http://pawws.secapl.com/C_bin/home.cgi

☐ **QUOTECOM DATA SERVICE**

This location is a free source of selected market data on topics such as stocks, commodities, futures, mutual funds, money market funds, and indexes. Access to more detailed information is available on a fee basis.

FTP   ftp.quote.com
Telnet   quote.com
Web   http://www.quote.com

☐ **TAXING TIMES**

This Web site has Canadian, U.S., and state tax information, including forms and codes.

Web   http://scubed.com/

Best Bets: Foreign Business and International Trade

☐ **AJBS-L**

This discussion group is an electronic forum for the Association of Japanese Business Studies.

Email   listserv@ncsuvm.cc.ncsu.edu

☐ **BASIC GUIDE TO EXPORTING**

This guide was created by the U.S. Department of Commerce to help potential exporters of American products.

Gopher   umslvma.umsl.edu:70/00/library/govdocs/expguide/eg_desc
Web   http://maingate.net/us-exports/bge.html

☐ **COUNTRY REPORTS ON ECONOMIC POLICY AND TRADE PRACTICES**

This source is derived from the CD-ROM National Trade Data Bank and contains economic, regulatory, and political information on foreign countries.

Gopher   umslvma.umsl.edu:70/00/library/govdocs/crpt/crpt0067

☐ **INTERNATIONAL BUSINESS PRACTICES**

This document provides trade information for exporters on 117 countries.

Gopher   umslvma.umsl.edu:70/00/library/govdocs/ibpa

☐ **JAPAN INFORMATION**

This Gopher site gives information on the culture, economy, society, foreign relations, and government of Japan.

Gopher   gan.ncc.go.jp:70/11/JAPAN

Best Bets: Government Publications and Legal Resources

☐ **CALIFORNIA STATE SENATE LEGISLATIVE DATABASE**

This site provides information on California legislation, including the text and history of bills for the current session. It also has the full text of the California Code and links to federal legislative information.

Gopher   sen.ca.gov/

☐ **DEFENSELINK**

DefenseLink contains news releases, contract award announcements (for awards of $5 million or more), and other current information from the U.S. Department of Defense.

Web   http://www.dtic.dla.mil/defenselink

☐ **FEDWORLD INFORMATION NETWORK** (National Technical Information Service)

According to its homepage, "The goal of NTIS FedWorld is to provide a one-stop location for the public to locate, order, and have delivered to them U.S. Government information." In its World-Wide Web format, it provides up-to-date links to many government sources.

Web   http://www.fedworld.gov/
Telnet   fedworld.gov

☐ **INTERNET SOURCES OF GOVERNMENT INFORMATION**, 2ND EDITION, 1994

This is a complete electronic bibliography of over 320 sites with government-produced information.

Email   mail-server@rtfm.mit.edu
              In the body of the message, type:
                  send usenet/news.answers/us-govt-net-pointers/part1
FTP   una.hh.lib.umich.edu/inetdirsstacks/government:gumprecht
              una.hh.lib.umich.edu/user:anonymous/password:*your email address*
Gopher   una.hh.lib.umich.edu:70/00/inetdirsstacks/government%3Agumprecht

☐ **LEGAL INFORMATION INSTITUTE** (Cornell University)

LII provides links to many business law-related sources.

Gopher telnet.law.cornell.edu

Telnet telnet.law.cornell.edu (login as "gopher")

Web http://www.law.cornell.edu/

☐ **MARVEL** (Library of Congress)

MARVEL is an excellent source for locating the full text of federal bills and laws, legislative histories, and regulations. It also is a gateway for finding grant information and other government-related information located in publications such as the *Catalog of Federal Domestic Assistance.* The "Government Information" option allows the user to select information from all levels of government and provides access to electronic information from agencies such as the Consumer Product Safety Commission, the Small Business Administration, the Food and Drug Administration, and other government bodies that produce business-related publications.

Gopher marvel.loc.gov:70/1

Telnet marvel.loc.gov (login as "marvel")

☐ **THOMAS** (Library of Congress)

THOMAS provides legislative and Congressional information for the 103rd and 104th Congresses, including the full text and legislative history of bills, resolutions, and statutes.

Telnet thomas.loc.gov (login as "thomas")

Web http://www.wlu.edu/law/lib

☐ **WASHINGTON AND LEE LAW LIBRARY SYSTEM** (Virginia)

This location is a good site for finding many business-related and legal information sources, such as trade treaties, the *Federal Register, Commerce Business Daily*, bill information, and thousands of full-text documents.

Gopher liberty.uc.wlu.edu:70/11/library/law

Web http://www.wlu.edu/law/lib

☐ **WHITEHOUSE HOMEPAGE**

Besides allowing you to hear Socks the cat meow, this Web page provides linkage to the numerous executive branch network sites that are growing in number every day.

Web http://www.whitehouse.gov

Best Bets: Management

☐ **CNI-MANAGEMENT**
(COALITION FOR NETWORKED INFORMATION MANAGEMENT)
CNI-MANAGEMENT is a discussion group dealing with the teaching and training of managers.
Email   listserv@cni.org

☐ **THE MANAGEMENT ARCHIVE**
This archive contains a variety of management-related publications, including working papers, recent calls for papers, teaching materials, and announcements of upcoming conferences.
Gopher   ursus.jun.alaska.edu/

☐ **ESBDC-L** (Small Business Development Centers List)
ESBDC-L is a listserv devoted to promoting the exchange of ideas on the management of small business and covers topics such as products, cost sharing, performance evaluation, and industry-related issues.
Email   listserv@ferris81.bit

☐ **QUALITY** (TQM IN MANUFACTURING AND SERVICE INDUSTRIES)
This listserv provides an electronic forum for discussing TQM in both the service and manufacturing industries.
Email   listserv@pucc.princeton.edu

Best Bets: Marketing Information

☐ **ELMAR**
Elmar is a moderated academic list for the discussion of marketing and marketing research.
Email   elmar-request@columbia.edu

☐ **THE GALLUP ORGANIZATION WORLD WIDE WEB SERVER**
This Web site is a growing source of Gallup Poll results.
Web   http://www.gallup.com/index.html

☐ **GLOBMKT**
Members of this forum discuss global marketing issues.
Email   listserv@ukcc.uky.edu

☐ **MARKETING TO CONSUMERS, AN OUTLINE**

This source gives an overview on how to market products.

Web   http://turnpike.net/metro/tuvok/index.html

☐ **MOUSETRACKS**

This Web site covers the development of marketing on the Internet. It includes "The List of Marketing Lists," which provides a variety of addresses for marketing-related discussion groups.

Web   http://nsns.com/MouseTracks/

☐ **NEWPROD**

A discussion list on the new product development process for both goods and services.

Email   majordomo@world.std.com

☐ **UPCLOSE DEMOGRAPHIC SUMMARIES 1994**

Upclose provides some free summary demographic information and more detailed data for a fee. Useful in marketing plans.

Web   http://www.digimark.net:80/upclose/demomenu/demomenu.htm

Best Bets: Operations and Statistical Methods

☐ **COMPUTATIONAL ECONOMICS, SARA**

This site contains general information on books and working papers and provides links to other Net locations dealing with computational economics.

Gopher   gopher.sara.nl

Web   http://www.sara.nl

☐ **DISCRETE MATHEMATICS AND THEORETICAL COMPUTER SCIENCE** (DIMACS)

Funded by the National Science Foundation, this homepage provides information on discrete mathematics and theoretical computer science.

Web   http://dimacs.rutgers.edu/

☐ **STATLIB** (Carnegie Mellon University)

STATLIB acts as a gateway to statistical programs, data, and other quantitative material.

Web   http://lib.stat.cmu.edu/

Best Bets: Personnel, Human Resources

☐ **ACADEMIC POSITION NETWORK**

This Gopher provides online announcements of faculty, staff, and administrative openings in academia.

Gopher   wcni.cis.umn.edu:11111/

☐ **HRD-L@MIZZOU1.BITNET** (THE HUMAN RESOURCE DEVELOPMENT GROUP)

This discussion group focuses on matters relating to personnel development.

Email   listserv@mizzou1.missouri.edu

☐ **ONLINE CAREER CENTER (OCC AT MSEN)**

The OCC provides access to job seekers' resumes and employers' job openings.

Gopher   occ.com/
Web   http://www.occ.com/

Glossary

address	Unique number or name that identifies a computer on the Internet.
anonymous FTP	Computer site that allows outside users access without having an account. Guest users enter "anonymous" at the login prompt, and then enter their email address at the password prompt.
archie	Program for locating anonymous FTP sites on the Internet.
bookmark	Gopher tool for saving useful Internet addresses for future connections.
client	Computer connecting to another computer (a server).
FTP	File Transfer Protocol: Method for transferring files from one computer to another.
Gopher	Protocol developed at the University of Minnesota that provides standardized presentation of Internet services such as Telnet and FTP.
host	Computer providing centralized services.
HTML	HyperText Markup Language: Marked text that allows the user of the World-Wide Web to click on highlighted words and connect to a new location.
Internet	Global network of networks based on the TCP/IP protocol and provides email, file transfer, and remote login functions.
listserv/listserver	Automatic email system that allows online discussion groups and forums.
login	Connect to a remote computer.
Mosaic	Software that allows the user to navigate the Internet in graphics mode and supports the use of graphic images, sounds, and moving pictures.
"Net"	The Internet (colloquial)
Network	Linked system that allows computers to communicate and share resources.
protocol	Uniform rules that computers use to communicate with each other.
server	Computer on a network that provides services to users or clients who have logged in.

TCP/IP	Transmission Control Protocol/Internet Protocol: Uniform rules, or protocols, that are used on the Internet.
Telnet	Method of connecting to another computer and operating databases residing on that computer.
Veronica	Software used to search Gopher sites by keywords.
World Wide Web	Hypertext representation of the Internet. Sometimes called WWW, W^3, or Web.

Quick Guide to Telnet, FTP, and Gopher Commands

Telnet Commands

`telnet <machine address>`	opens connection
`open <machine address>`	opens connection if you are already in Telnet mode
`^c`	takes you out of current activity
`quit`	exits Telnet
`^]`	if all else fails, will usually disconnect

FTP Commands

`ftp` [or] `open <machine address>`	opens connection
`ls`	shows files & subdirectories of current directory
`dir`	similar to `ls`, only shows more detail
`cd <directory name>`	changes directory
`get <filename>`	transfers remote file. You can change the local file name by appending new name to the command string (e.g., `get <remote file> locfile`)
`get <filename> |more`	allows you to read files on a remote computer, particularly important for README and index files
`binary`	allows you to transfer non-ASCII files
`bye` [or] `quit`	logs you out of a remote computer

Gopher Commands

Navigating commands:

Use the arrow keys or their character equivalents to move around.

`right, return`	"enter"/display current item
`left, u`	"exit" current item/go up a level
`down`	move to next line
`up`	move to previous line
`>, +, Pgdwn, space`	view next page of menu selections
`<, -, Pgup, b`	view previous page of menu selections
`0-9`	go to a specific line
`m`	go back to the main menu

Gopher Commands
(continued)

Bookmarks:

a	add current item to the bookmark list
A	add current directory/search to bookmark list
v	view bookmark list
d	delete a bookmark/directory entry

Other commands:

q	quit with prompt
Q	quit unconditionally
s	save current item to a file
S	save current menu listing to a file
d	download a file
r	go to root menu of current item
R	go to root menu of current menu
=	display technical information about current item
^	display technical information about current directory
o	open a new gopher server
O	change options
/	search for an item in the menu
n	find next search item

Background Reading: A Bibliography

Butler, Mark. *How to Use the Internet.* Emeryville, Calif.: Ziff-Davis Press, 1994.

Cronin, Mary J. *Doing Business on the Internet: How the Electronic Highway Is Transforming American Companies.* New York: Van Nostrand Reinhold, 1994.

Dern, Daniel P. *The Internet Guide for New Users.* New York: McGraw-Hill, 1994.

Estrada, Susan. *Connecting to the Internet: A Buyer's Guide.* Sebastopol, Calif.: O'Reilly & Associates, 1993.

Gibbs, Mark, and Richard Smith. *Navigating the Internet.* Indianapolis: Sam's Publishing, 1993.

Hahan, Harley, and Rick Stout. *The Internet Yellow Pages.* Berkeley, Calif.: Osborne-McGraw Hill, 1994.

Jaffe, Lee David. *Introducing the Internet: A Trainer's Workshop.* Berkeley, Calif.: Library Solutions Press, 1994.

Kehoe, Brenden P. *Zen and the Art of the Internet: A Beginner's Guide.* 3d ed. Englewood, N.J.: Prentice-Hall, 1994.

Krol, Ed. *The Whole Internet User's Guide and Catalog.* 2d ed. Sebastopol, Calif.: O'Reilly and Associates, 1994.

Levine, John R., and Carol Baroudi. *Internet for Dummies.* San Mateo, Calif.: IDG Books Worldwide, 1994.

Quarterman, John S., and Smoot Carl-Mitchell. *The Internet Connection: System Connectivity and Configuration.* Reading, Mass. : Addison-Wesley, 1994.

Robison, David F.W. *All About Internet FTP: Learning and Teaching to Transfer Files on the Internet.* Berkeley, Calif.: Library Solutions Press, 1994.

Tennant, Roy, John Ober, and Anne Lipow. *Crossing the Internet Threshold: An Instructional Handbook.* 2d ed. Berkeley, Calif.: Library Solutions Press, 1994.

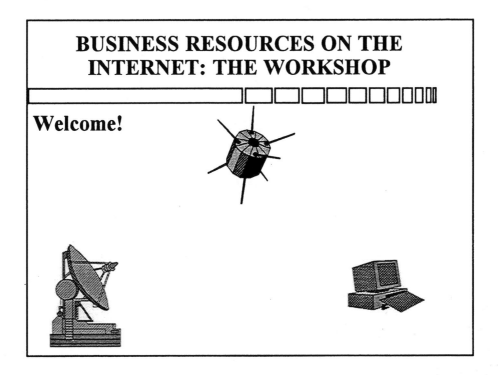

BEFORE YOU START THE WORKSHOP. . .

1. Have you completed the pre-workshop exercise in "Best Bets for
   Exploration..." (*Ready Reference Guides*, page 3)? If not, please do that now.

2. If you come across a term you do not understand, look up its meaning in the
   Glossary (*Ready Reference Guides*, page 18).

3. When you are ready to explore the Internet on your own, you'll find a handy
   reminder of commands in "Quick Guide to Telnet, FTP, and Gopher
   Commands" (*Ready Reference Guides*, page 20).

4. To learn more about the Internet than is within the scope of this book, consult
   the references in "Background Reading: A Bibliography" (*Ready Reference
   Guides*, page 22).

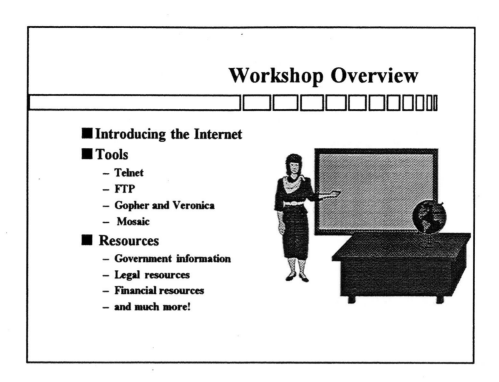

Workshop Overview

■ **Introducing the Internet**
■ **Tools**
- Telnet
- FTP
- Gopher and Veronica
- Mosaic

■ **Resources**
- Government information
- Legal resources
- Financial resources
- and much more!

OVERVIEW OF A MOVING TARGET

You can't escape it. Every day newspapers, magazines, television, and radio are bombarding us with the news that the information superhighway is under construction and that we should all be prepared to hit the road.

Along with this heralding of a new information age comes the proclamation that the Internet, the once-private domain of academics, is now open to the commercial world. As pointed out in *PC Magazine*, the arrival of alternative connections to the Internet that are not government supported have opened a door that for years had been closed by the National Science Foundation's "acceptable use policy" against the commercial use of the Internet ("Business in Cyberspace," in *PC Magazine*, August 1994). For a relatively small monthly fee, businesses and the public they hope to reach can now be connected to the Internet. Predictions of more and more businesses merging onto the information highway with a vengeance are mounting daily. For most businesses, this form of communication promises to be a two-way street: a way to advertise their products to potential customers and, at the same time, a means for obtaining information for making sound business decisions.

Just as the use and users of the Internet are rapidly changing, so is the face of the Net. Programs such as Gopher, Veronica, Archie, Lynx, Mosaic, and Netscape are changing the appearance of this form of communication at a fast pace. Whereas once you had to have a love for Unix and some fairly arcane commands, now menu-driven and graphical user interfaces (GUI, pronounced "gooey") have opened up the cyberspace to huge numbers of users who a few years ago would not have dared venture into such a technologically threatening environment.

This book is designed to prepare users of the Internet for an ever-changing network environment. It provides step-by-step directions for using Telnet, FTP, Archie, Gopher, Veronica, and Mosaic—commonly available Internet tools used to locate, read, and save business and economics information, and it covers what you need to know to explore the Net on your own.

The presentation is divided into various modules. This first module contains an overview of the development of the Internet, the business use of the Net, and explanations of various tools used on the Internet. Following the introductory portion are detailed examples of how to use email, Telnet, FTP, Gopher, and World Wide Web to locate information. You may follow these examples while online to get the feel for how the Internet works. After trying out any tool, be sure to refer to the first section in this book for "Best Bets for Exploration," an annotated list of business, government, and economics sources that you can use to practice your skills, explore, and obtain informaton. Also in the preliminary section is a "Quick Guide to FTP, Telnet, and Gopher Commands," as well as "Background Reading: A Bibliography."

This book does not cover how to get connected to the Internet. The software, hardware, and means of gaining access to the Internet are well-covered in other introductory works, several of which are listed in "Background Reading." Refer to these books for information on modems, communications software, and network providers.

MODULE *1* : Introducing the Internet

This section covers background information about the Internet. If you already have Internet access, read articles about the Internet in the daily press, understand Internet addresses and URLs, and are eager to get your fingers working, skip this section and go to Module 2.

What is the Internet?

Trends and developments

Number of commercial networks

Commercial use of the Internet

How to get access

What you can do on the Internet

Network addresses

Uniform Resource Locators (URLs)

Those frustrating moments

Review

BUSINESS RESOURCES ON THE INTERNET

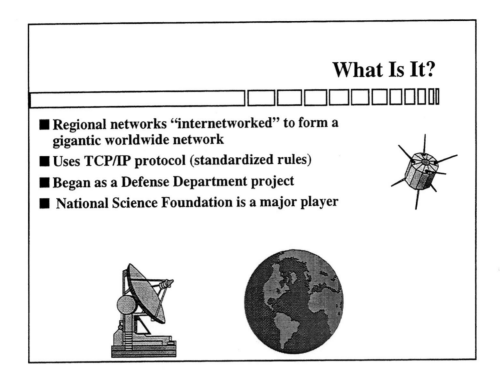

What Is It?

- Regional networks "internetworked" to form a gigantic worldwide network
- Uses TCP/IP protocol (standardized rules)
- Began as a Defense Department project
- National Science Foundation is a major player

WHAT IS THE INTERNET?

The Internet is a gigantic collection of networks that have been "internetted" or linked together. It allows local networks to communicate with other local networks around the globe.

The Internet uses TCP/IP (Transfer Control Protocol/ Internet Protocol), a special "protocol" or standardized set of rules that allows different types of computer platforms (PCs, Macs, Unix, CMS, etc.) to talk with each other.

The network evolved out of a system that was developed for the U.S. Department of Defense to communicate among research sites. By the late 1980s, the National Science Foundation assumed responsibility for the Internet and established five supercomputer sites in various parts of the United States to handle the electronic traffic. Under the NSF's guidance, the Net supported enhanced communications and academic-oriented research resources. However, the NSF prohibited the use of the Net for commercial purposes until the early 1990s, when commercial access was allowed.

The Internet is a voluntary community of networks, with little formal regulation. The issuance and format of addresses and some guidelines covering inappropriate uses of the Net are controlled centrally, but on the whole it is an unregulated system.

Trends

- ■ Software such as Gopher, Archie, Veronica, and Mosaic are making it easier to search
- ■ Fee-based access providers are on the rise
- ■ Government initiatives support enlarging and commercializing
- ■ Commercial users are growing in number

TRENDS AND DEVELOPMENTS

There is an ongoing trend toward making the Internet easier to use and more accessible by the general public. With menu- and graphic-based front-end software (the software used to connect to the Internet), you have been relieved of the need to learn the cryptic commands that were used in the early days of the network and that still underlie the interface to the Internet. As you will see later in this workshop, using menu-driven programs such as Gopher provides much easier access to the resources on the Net.

Whereas a few years ago the only way to access the Internet was through a research institute or university computer center, private companies are now offering the general public an opportunity to dial in to the Internet on a subscription basis. For a relatively modest monthly fee, you can obtain an account on the Net. Several references in "Background Reading" (page 21) give advice on how to go about finding a network provider.

With the 1992 election of Bill Clinton and Al Gore, the federal government has placed a major emphasis on promoting and establishing a national information policy that includes an Internet-type network that can be used for research, defense, and commercial purposes.

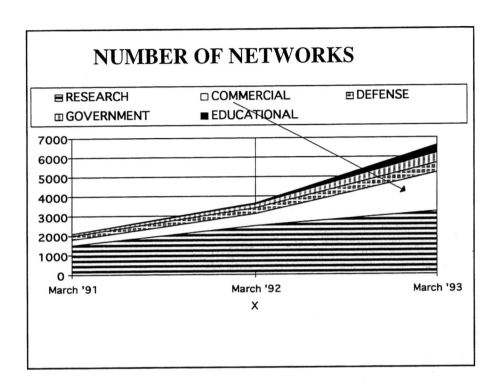

NUMBER OF COMMERCIAL NETWORKS

In the two-year period between March 1991 and March 1993, the number of commercial networks increased by more than 600%. It was by far the fastest-growing segment of the Internet.

In August 1994, *INTERNET Info,* an online service that monitors Internet developments, reported that of 2064 publicly traded companies with sales in excess of $400 million, 38% have some form of Internet presence.

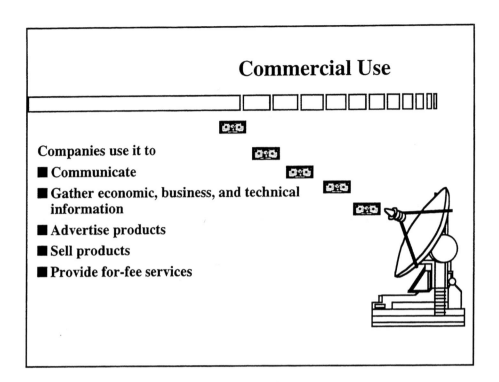

Commercial Use

Companies use it to
■ Communicate
■ Gather economic, business, and technical information
■ Advertise products
■ Sell products
■ Provide for-fee services

COMMERCIAL USE OF THE INTERNET

Commercial use of the Internet has been growing in a number of different ways. Companies find email an effective way of communicating among their employees. They also use the Internet to gather information on the economy and the business world in general, as well as to plan their own future or obtain information on markets and product development.

Many firms are capitalizing on the development of the Net by creating products and services for Internet users. New services enabling you to buy software packages, online magazines, advertising space, products from online catalogs, and other commercial ventures are cropping up every day.

Companies such as Mead Data Central, distributor of the LEXIS/NEXIS database, are using the Internet as an alternative method for their clients to access their information. By having an Internet address for their customers to use, they can provide an inexpensive and fast method for using their electronic products.

Also, products can be ordered over the Internet. Indeed, in August 1994, Pizza Hut announced that it had set up an Internet account so customers can browse their menu and order home delivery.

How Do You Get Access?

- Through a server connected to the Net
- Through a hardwired machine, such as workstations on a college campus
- By dialing up through a modem to a networked computer
- By subscribing to a local Internet provider

HOW TO GET ACCESS

Your workstation has to be connected to the Internet through a server (the computer that is connected to the Internet). Some workstations are directly wired into the server, while others use a modem to dial in to a server using telephone lines.

Most colleges and universities have a mix of hardwired and dialup systems.

Local private companies are setting up servers that, for a small monthly fee, allow you to dial in and use the Internet. Some providers charge a flat fee for unlimited access to the Net or for a fixed number of hours; others charge extra depending on some aspect of usage, for example, use during peak hours or use of certain network services.

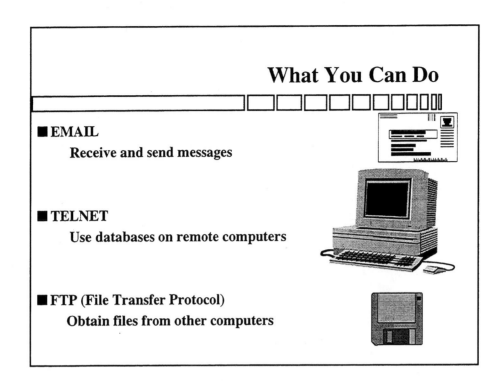

What You Can Do

■ **EMAIL**
   Receive and send messages

■ **TELNET**
   Use databases on remote computers

■ **FTP (File Transfer Protocol)**
   Obtain files from other computers

WHAT YOU CAN DO ON THE INTERNET

Email allows you to send and receive messages on the Net. It is a form of rapid, inexpensive communication between two or more people.

Telnet allows you to connect to a remote computer and run programs or use systems remotely, as if the machine were on your desk.

FTP, or File Transfer Protocol, allows you to locate and download files that reside on remote systems.

Email, Telnet, and FTP are the three basic functions on the Net. Although they are separate tools, programs such as Gopher and Mosaic combine them under a common interface.

You will examine these tools and practice using them later in this workshop.

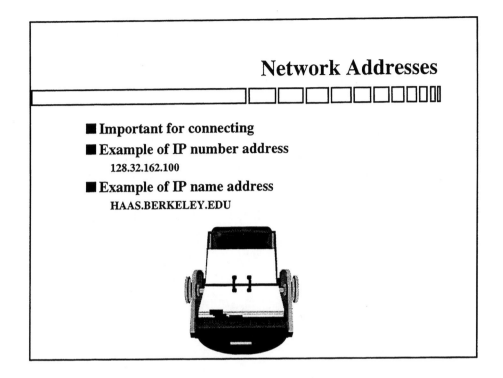

NETWORK ADDRESSES

Computers on the Net are assigned addresses that are used to reach the right destination.

As the examples on the screen show, each computer on the Net is given a unique *numerical* address and a unique *name* address that represents that IP number address. Using either one of the addresses on the screen, you would connect to the same computer located at the Haas School of Business at the University of California, Berkeley.

URL

- Standardized Internet address citation
- Used in navigating through the World Wide Web
- Examples of URLs
  - ftp://tuna.berkeley.edu/public
  - gopher://infolib.berkeley.edu
  - http://riskweb.bus.utexas.edu/finweb.htm [1]
  - telnet://fedworld.gov

UNIFORM RESOURCE LOCATORS (URLs)

The URL (sometimes pronounced "you-are-el," sometimes "earl") is a citation method that standardizes the way the location of an item is described. Each URL gives a lot of information.

You can tell immediately what type of connection will be available at the address by the prefix that appears before the actual address. In the examples above,

•ftp:// is for a file transfer protocol location.

•gopher:// is an address for a Gopher system.

•http:// is for a site using hypertext, usually a World-Wide Web connection.

•telnet:// is to a Telnet location.

After the double slash (//) comes the Internet address.

A single slash (/) in a URL indicates that what follows is a file name or a progression down a hierarchy from directory to subdirectory(ies) to a file. In the http:// example above, the "/finweb.htm" portion of this URL is a file located at the Internet address "riskweb.bus.utexas.edu". These file names are important because they get you directly to the information that you need—through layers of directories right down to the specific file.

How do you use URLs? If you are using a World-Wide Web client, such as Mosaic (about which you will learn in Module 6), key the entire URL. If you are using Telnet or FTP, key only the address appearing after the double slash.

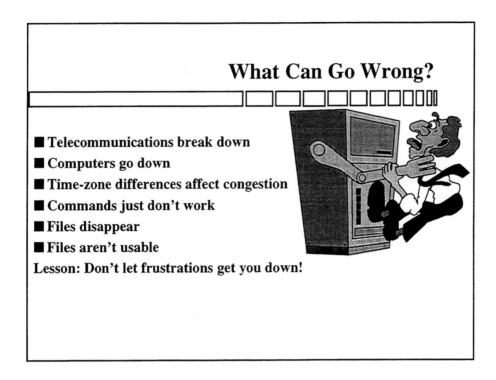

What Can Go Wrong?

- Telecommunications break down
- Computers go down
- Time-zone differences affect congestion
- Commands just don't work
- Files disappear
- Files aren't usable

Lesson: Don't let frustrations get you down!

THOSE FRUSTRATING MOMENTS

Complex operations are taking place in a still-evolving system when you use the Net, so it is hardly surprising that many things can go awry.

•Telecommunications problems can cut you off from your destination. A broken router, a satellite failing, a cable breaking, or a relay station going down are only a few links in the telecommunications chain that can break. With the tremendous increase in users on the Net, communications systems can be quickly swamped, clogged, and excruciatingly slow.

•Host computers (the computer to which you are trying to connect) are often taken offline for maintenance and repair. They also can break down and be out of commission for extended periods.

•You may be trying to use a database that is located in a time zone where it is the peak-use period and the system is overloaded with users.

•For one reason or another, commands just don't work. For no apparent reason, even the disconnect command of last resort, "^]" (Control and right bracket keys), does not respond and you are stuck.

•It is also not unusual to use a particular resource one week, and when you try to use it again the next week, it no longer is available. Since the Internet is a voluntary, cooperative enterprise, there are no guarantees of how long a resource will be maintained and made available.

•Files that you locate and download may just not be usable when you get them back.

The point is that using the Internet can be a frustrating experience, especially if you aren't anticipating these problems. But don't give up. If something goes wrong and you try in vain to fix it, you can always turn off your machine and try again at a later time.

Review

In this first module, you have been given a brief history of the development of the Internet, with special emphasis on the growing commercial use. You have been introduced to how one gains access to the Internet, shown what one can do once on the Net, and taught what network addresses and URLs are. And finally you have been given some examples of what can go wrong. Now you will begin exploring some of the tools for navigating the Internet.

MODULE *2* : Email

Uses of email

How to read email addresses

Finding an email address

Discussion groups

How to join a listserv

Exercise: Join a business discussion group

Review

Uses of Email

■ **Send messages quickly, inexpensively anywhere in the world**

■ **Follow and contribute to group discussions on every topic imaginable**

USES OF EMAIL

Email enables you to send messages to others on the Net anywhere in the world. Features such as distribution lists allow you to communicate one message to multiple recipients simultaneously.

Also, you can subscribe to discussion groups, which allow you to particpate in the exchange of ideas and news on particular topics.

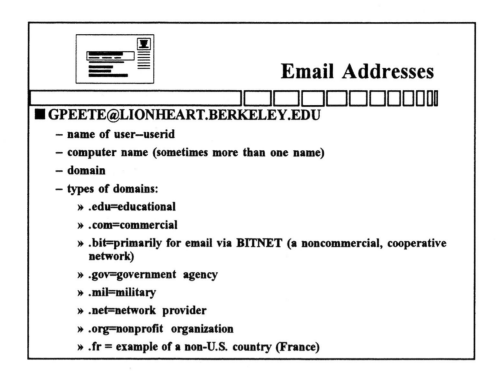

Email Addresses

■ **GPEETE@LIONHEART.BERKELEY.EDU**
 – name of user--userid
 – computer name (sometimes more than one name)
 – domain
 – types of domains:
  » .edu=educational
  » .com=commercial
  » .bit=primarily for email via BITNET (a noncommercial, cooperative network)
  » .gov=government agency
  » .mil=military
  » .net=network provider
  » .org=nonprofit organization
  » .fr = example of a non-U.S. country (France)

HOW TO READ EMAIL ADDRESSES

In the example above, the first element, "gpeete," is the userid, which is an example of the unique account name given to each user of the Net.

Next comes the name of the host computer and the institution where the computer is located, separated by a period. This is where messages are stored until read and deleted by the person owning the account.

Finally comes the domain, which is a three-letter code for the type of subnetwork that the host computer operates in the United States or, in the case of non-U.S. countries, an abbreviation for the nation where the host is located.

The example here is for a user at a host computer named lionheart, located at UC Berkeley, which is connected to the educational subnetwork.

Finding Email Addresses

- **Finger command**
- **Electronic phone directories**
- **Ask the person directly**

FINDING AN EMAIL ADDRESS

There are various tools for finding someone's email address, and since none is complete, you may need to try more than one.

If you are on the same host, you can use a "finger" command by typing at the command prompt **finger** followed by the person's name.

Another method is to connect to one of the electronic directories of email users such as "netfind." Not all institutions or users are represented on this directory, so it does not always work. To access netfind, at the command prompt use the telnet command and the host address as follows:

telnet bruno.cs.colorado.edu

Printed directories are also available, such as the *Internet White Pages*. Unfortunately, even with 100,000 entries, this directory is extremely incomplete.

Sometimes the easiest way to find out someone's email address is simply to ask them. Use an old, tried-and-true communication device: the telephone.

Types of Discussion Groups

- **Newsgroups**
  - Messages are distributed to host servers
  - You must go to a host server to read messages
- **Mailservers**
  - You must subscribe to the discussion group
  - Subscriptions are managed by programs (listserv, majordomo, etc.)
  - Messages are sent to your emailbox
- **Moderated and unmoderated groups**

DISCUSSION GROUPS

There are countless electronic discussion groups on the Internet that allow people with a common interest to share ideas and information. The range of topics for these discussion groups—also known as lists, conferences, or forums—is endless and as diverse as comic book heroes, finance, real estate, gourmet cooking, and business librarianship. They come most commonly in two forms: newsgroups (or Usenet News) and mailservers. Some discussion groups exist in both forms. In both, users can send messages and the messages can be read by all users. Mailservers are sometimes moderated, where someone monitors the messages to make sure that the mail going out to subscribers is on a topic appropriate to the purpose of the discussion group. Others are unmoderated and messages go out to others on the mailserver unexamined.

A principal difference between a newsgroup and a mailserver is the way messages are accessed. Newsgroups are comparable to bulletin boards in that they distribute their messages to host servers and you must login to a host server to read the postings. By contrast, mailservers send messages from each contributor to the entire subscriber list.

Mailservers are managed by software that handles subscriptions and other administrative matters. There are several list-managing programs—among them Listserv, Majordomo, and Listprocessor, to name three. And of these three, probably the most fully developed and common is Listserv. The names and addresses of some of the more prominent business and economics listservs are included in the "Best Bets for Exploration" list.

Subscribing to a Listserv

- **Send email to LISTSERV address, and. . .**
  - leave the subject line blank
  - in the body of the message type:
    subscribe <name of LISTSERV>
- **LISTSERV will respond with**
  - rules for appropriate use
  - how to particpate
  - how to unsubscribe
  - how to customize your subscription
  - how to access archived material (if available)

HOW TO JOIN A LISTSERV

To subscribe to a forum described as a listserv or newsletter, use the email address given for *subscriptions:* listserv@<list host address>

Do not enter anything in the subject line, and type the following in the message body:

subscribe <name of LISTSERV>

The LISTSERV will respond with an important message that explains how to use the system, including how to send messages to the list, what is and is not appropriate, and other information that you may want to save for later reference.

Before you decide to subscribe to a LISTSERV, be aware that the more active lists can generate tremendous numbers of messages per week that can end up in your email box.

Generally, to stop receiving messages from a listserv you send the following to the subscription address:

unsubscribe <name of LISTSERV>

Caution: There are two addresses pertaining to a listserv: one is for sending messages *about* your subscription; it goes to *listserv*@<list node address>. The other is for sending messages to the subscribers and goes to *<listname>*@<list node address>. Many people mistakenly send a "subscribe" or "unsubscribe" message, or any of the many other commands related to managing their subscription, to the "listname" address, in which case they often receive scolding messages from subscribers who regard such mistakes as thoughtless and wasting their valuable time.

EXERCISE: JOIN A BUSINESS DISCUSSION GROUP

In this exercise you will join a discussion group. You may follow the example below, or choose a listserv that interests you from the "Best Bets for Exploration" section. If you choose the latter, substitute your listserv name and host site for the those in italics in the example. We will subscribe to ESBDC-L, a discussion group pertaining to small businesses (page 15).

1. Send an email message to the listserv.

    Example:

    To: majordomo@world.std.com

    Leave the subject line blank

    In the message block, type only:

    subscribe *newprod*

    Send the message.

    You will receive two messages generated automatically by the listserv program: one that tells you your message was received, and another that welcomes you to the group and gives you information about its purpose and how to perform various subscriber activities.

2. Watch your mailbox for the next few days to see what mail you get from the group.

3. Unsubscribe (if you so wish) by sending another message to the listserv.

    Example:

    To: majordomo@world.std.com

    In the message block, type:

    unsubscribe *newprod*

Review

You now have a grounding in email basics: you know the elements of an email address; you know the common ways of finding the email address of a friend or colleague, and you can join an electronic discussion group. With this information, you can participate in what is perhaps the most remarkable benefit of the Internet, one that has the potential to break down geographical, political, and social walls: the world-wide, people-to-people communications network.

MODULE *3* : Telnet

Basic facts about Telnet

Basic Telnet commands

Using Telnet to access business information
via the Library of Congress

    Example: LC MARVEL
                  ↓
                  Business Reference Tools
                  ↓
                  Entrepreneurs Reference Guide to
                  Small Business Information

Using Telnet to access legal resources
at Washburn Law Library

    Example: Legal References—
                  The Virtual Reference Desk
                  ↓
                  Business/Banking Reference Notes
                  ↓
                  President Signing Small Business
                  Reauthorization Act (press release)

Review

Telnet (Remote Login)

- Use remote databases as if you were there
- Some sites require passwords to access
- Some are free, some charge

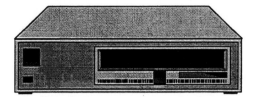

BASIC FACTS ABOUT TELNET

Telnet allows you to login to a remote computer and interactively use programs on that computer. Once logged in to the remote site, you can operate that computer just as if you were at that location.

Some sites require passwords to use their networked programs. Many sites offer free access. Commercial information distributors, such as Mead Data Central's LEXIS/NEXIS and the Dow Jones News Retrieval database, allow you to use Telnet to access their information center, but require a password for billing purposes. Connecting to a remote computer via Telnet rather than through a direct-dial telephone connection saves you telecommunications costs.

Remember, once you establish a Telnet connection, you will be operating the remote computer using the commands required by that remote network.

Telnet Commands

- telnet <machine address>   Opens connection
- open <machine address>   Opens connection if you are already in telnet
- ^c   Takes you out of current activity
- ^]   If all else fails
- quit Exits telnet

BASIC TELNET COMMANDS

The command used to make the connection is the word *telnet* followed by the Internet address for the computer to which you want to connect. You can use either the name address or numeric address. For instance, to connect to the computer located at the Walter A. Haas School of Business at the University of California at Berkeley you can type either **telnet haas.berkeley.edu** or **telnet 128.32.159.13.**

> *Note:* Name addresses are more commonly used. They are easier to remember than numeric addresses and are usually more stable. That is, a site may move a database to a machine with a different numerical address but will keep the same name address.

If you type the command **telnet** and do not put an address after it, the command prompt will change to "telnet>." Now you are in the Telnet program (as indicated by the new prompt). To connect to the remote site, you must now give the command **open** followed by the name or number of the system you want to use, for example, **open haas.berkeley.edu**.

Once you are connected, often there will be a message that tells you how to interrupt a process, usually "^c" or "^]".

You may also be asked to provide the type of terminal or terminal emulation that you are using (for example, vt100). Your terminal emulation type is set up in your telecommunications software.

To exit from your Telnet session, type **quit** and you will be returned to your local computer network.

Using Telnet to Access
Business Information via
the Library Congress

```
                                                                  


                                                                  


                                                                  


               To return to the menu system type 'menu' at any haas prompt.




       haas 59 ~> telnet marvel.loc.gov
```

Note: In the above screen, the message in the center and the prompt "haas59~>" are local to the machine used for this demonstration. Your screen will look different. However, what you see *after* the prompt is what you should type.

When you use Telnet, you are using the Internet to login to a remote computer and use databases that reside on that computer. Unlike using a Gopher interface, a Telnet connection does not have a consistent appearance because you are using the software provided by the host computer (the computer to which you have connected).

To start, type **telnet** followed by the Internet address where you want to connect. In this case, you are logging in to a computer that resides at the Library of Congress with the address of marvel.loc.gov, so you type **telnet marvel.loc.gov** and hit the **<Enter >** or **<Return>** key.

Response to Telnet Command

```
haas 59 ~> telnet marvel.loc.gov
Trying 140.147.2.69...
Connected to rs7.loc.gov.
Escape character is '^]'.



AIX telnet (rs7)




AIX Version 3
(C) Copyrights by IBM and by others 1982, 1993.
login: marvel
```

At the top of this screen, you see that your Telnet command is attempting to connect to the Internet address 140.147.2.69, which is the numerical address for marvel.loc.gov.

When the connection is made, the message "Escape character is '^]'." appears. This statement is telling you that if your computer freezes for some reason, you can break the connection to the Library of Congress computer by pressing the **Control** key (signfied by ^) and the **right bracket** key (]) simultaneously.

> *Lesson*: Whenever you telnet to a computer, you need to note what the escape character sequence is so you can disconnect if there is a problem. Heavy traffic on the host computer or some other irregularity might cause slow or no response at all, so it is important to note how to escape from such a situation.

At the bottom of the screen, you are asked for a "login," which in this case is "marvel." Unfortunately, login commands, when required, have no standard format. Sometimes the host computer will provide it. However, often, including this case, you must have acquired the correct login sequence from another source, such as the "Best Bets For Exploration" list, one of the Ready Reference Guides in this book.

After you have entered the login command, the next screen (below) provides you with information on the type of software you will be using and the limitations that are placed on remote users of this computer. In this case, you are alerted to the limit on the number of Telnet users who are allowed to use the Library of Congress computer, and you are encouraged to use a Gopher connection, which does not have a limit on the number of simultaneous users.

To continue, press **<Enter>**.

```
Welcome to rs7.loc.gov (Library of Congress).
Last login: Wed Dec 14 00:50:30 1994 on pts/5 from 164.124.101.4
You are outside user number 5 (15 maximum).

                  WELCOME TO LC
MARVEL..........................................................
             Library of Congress
   Machine-Assisted Realization of the Virtual Electronic Library
...................................................................
   LC MARVEL is the Campus-Wide Information System for the Library of
Congress using Gopher software developed by the University of Minnesota.
   15 simultaneous connections are available through our courtesy TELNET
client from external sites (with the exception of the US Congress). We
highly recommend that you connect to this system using Gopher or other
client software or via the Gopher server at your site (the 15-user limit
does not apply to these access methods). Point to MARVEL.LOC.GOV, port 70.
Clearly, the Library of Congress bears NO responsibility for the quality
of information provided through other sites and computer systems.
...................................................................
Please forward your suggestions and reports of any technical problems to:
           lcmarvel@loc.gov..........................................................
          PRESS <RETURN> TO CONTINUE
```

You are now given a number of menu options that will lead you to information about Library of Congress services (2), copyright (5), the U.S. Congress (8), and much more. You are looking for business information, which falls in the category of "reference" information, so type **3<Enter >**.

```
You are outside user number 5 (15 maximum).
        Internet Gopher Information Client v2.0.14


            Library of Congress MARVEL
 --> 1.  About LC MARVEL/
     2.  Events, Facilities, Publications, and Services/
     3.  Research and Reference (Public Services)/
     4.  Libraries and Publishers (Technical Services)/
     5.  Copyright/
     6.  Library of Congress Online Systems/
     7.  Employee Information/
     8.  U.S. Congress/
     9.  Government Information/
     10. Global Electronic Library (by Subject)/
     11. Internet Resources/
     12. What's New on LC MARVEL/
     13. Search LC MARVEL Menus/
View item number: 3
```

Now type **7 <Enter>** to get to business information.

```
Internet Gopher Information Client v2.0.14


        Research and Reference (Public Services)


 --> 1.  Services to Researchers/
     2.  Reading Rooms of the Library of Congress (Under Construction)/
     3.  Reference Questions: Where to Write/
     4.  Library of Congress Online Information System (LOCIS)/
     5.  Librarian's Rolodex: Frequently Asked Questions/
     6.  LC Bibliographies and Guides (Under Construction)/
     7.  Online Business Information Network (Under Construction)/
     8.  Dance Heritage Coalition (Under Construction)/
     9.  LC Collections and Catalogs/
     10. Electronic Publications (Non-LC)/




View item number: 7
```

Next, type **4 <Enter>** to select the Business Information Tools option.

```
┌─────────────────────────────────────────────────────────────┐
│  Internet Gopher Information Client v2.0.14                   │
│                                                               │
│        Online Business Information Network (Under Construction)│
│                                                               │
│  -->  1.  Welcome                                             │
│       2.  Business Research Project News/                     │
│       3.  The Talkies (under construction)/                   │
│       4.  Business Information Tools/                         │
│       5.  Gateways/                                           │
│                                                               │
│                                                               │
│                                                               │
│                                                               │
│                                                               │
│  View item number: 4                                          │
│                                                               │
└─────────────────────────────────────────────────────────────┘
```

Now type **1 <Enter>** to choose the Business Reference Tools option.

```
┌─────────────────────────────────────────────────────────────┐
│  Internet Gopher Information Client v2.0.14                   │
│                                                               │
│                   Business Information Tools                  │
│                                                               │
│  -->  1.  Business Reference Tools/                           │
│       2.  Directory of Volunteer Experts/                     │
│       3.  Directory of Exceptional Projects/                  │
│       4.  Federal Programs and Services/                      │
│                                                               │
│                                                               │
│                                                               │
│                                                               │
│                                                               │
│  View item number: 1                                          │
│                                                               │
└─────────────────────────────────────────────────────────────┘
```

To use the business reference tools from the Library of Congress, type
1 <Enter>.

```
Business Reference Tools

 -->  1.  Reference Tools from the Library of Congress/
      2.  Tools from the James Jerome Hill Reference Library/

















View item number: 1
```

To view the Entrepreneur's Guide to Small Business Information, type
1<Enter>.

```
Internet Gopher Information Client v2.0.14

            Reference Tools from the Library of Congress

 -->  1.  Entrepreneur's Guide to Small Business Information
      2.  Financing Small Business Enterprises















View item number: 1
```

```
Entrepreneur's Guide to Small Business Information (75k)
,,,,,,,,,,,,,,,,,,,,,,,,,,,,,,,,,,,,,,,,,,,,,,,,,,,,,,,,,,,,,,,,,,,,,,,,,,,,,,,,,,,,,,,,,,,,,,,,,,,,,,,,,,,,,,,



                              THE
                ENTREPRENEUR'S REFERENCE GUIDE
                TO SMALL BUSINESS INFORMATION






                          Compiled by
                          the staff of
,,,,,,,,,,,,,,,,,,,,,,,,,,,,,,,,,,,,,,,,,,,,,,,,,,,,,,,,,,,,,,,,,,,,,,,,,,,,,,,,,,,,,,,,,,,,,,,,,,,,,,,,,,,,,,,

[Help: ?]  [Exit: u]  [Mail: m]  [PageDown: Space]
```

You are now at the title page of the guide (above), where you can see the size of the file is 75k. Since you have telneted into a location that is running a Gopher access program, the standard commands are listed at the bottom of the screen:

You can read the guide page by page by hitting the **space bar** to advance to each subsequent screen.

Or, if you need help, type **?** for options.

To email the entire document to your email address, type **m**.

For now, choose the remaining option, **u**, to go back (up) one level, thus exiting the document.

You can now explore this site on your own by choosing other menu options to move deeper into the layers of offerings, and getting to other menus by typing **u** to back out of your present menu.

When you are ready to disconnect completely and return to your home computer, type **q**.

Using Telnet to Access Legal Resources at Washburn Law Library

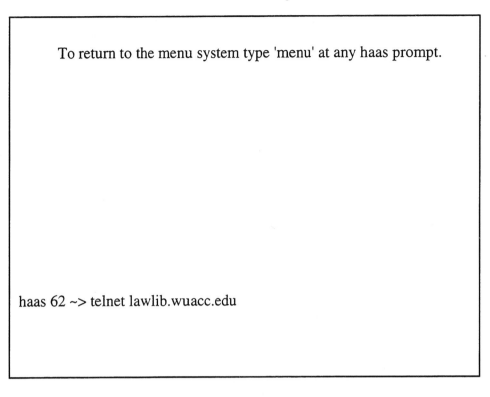

To return to the menu system type 'menu' at any haas prompt.

haas 62 ~> telnet lawlib.wuacc.edu

Let us imagine that a friend told you about a site, the Washburn Law Library, that focuses on legal information and contains good business information. Your friend also gave you the headings to choose once you reach the site, layer by layer: first "Legal Reference-The Virtual Reference Desk"; then "Business/Banking Reference Notes." To visit that site, at the prompt type **telnet** followed by the address **lawlib.wuacc.edu,** as shown above, and press **<Enter>**.

```
Trying 192.104.1.6...
Connected to lawlib.wuacc.edu.
Escape character is '^]'.


telnet (lawlib)



AIX Version 4
(C) Copyrights by IBM and by others 1982, 1994.
login: washlaw
```

At the top of the screen appears a message indicating the numerical address to which you are connecting. Once connected, you are given the escape character sequence that can be used if you get "hung up" and the computer locks up or stops responding. To complete the connection, type **washlaw** at the login prompt. As in the previous example, this command is not obvious; you would have to have found it in a secondary source, in this case, your friend, to get beyond this point.

The opening screen (below) gives you the logo of the Washburn Law Library, its addresses and telephone numbers, and a list of basic commands. To go to the next screen, press **<Enter>**.

```
WW   WW WW    AA      SSSSSSS HH    HH LL        AA WW     WW WW
WW WW WW    A A      SS      HH    HH LL         A A WW    WW WW
WW WW WW  AAAAAA SSSSS  HHHHHHHH LL      AAAAAA WW  WW WW
  WWW WWW   AA   AA     SS HH    HH LL      AA    AA WWW WWW
  WW WW     AA    AA SSSSSSS HH    HH LLLLLLLL AA    AA   WW WW


        Welcome to Washburn University
      School of Law Library Information System
              1700 College
              Topeka, KS 66621
          Voice: (913) 231-1010 ext 1341
              Fax: (913) 232-8087
          zzfolm@acc.wuacc.edu

        [1]Press ENTER to Continue


Commands: Use arrow keys to move, '?' for help, 'q' to quit, '<-' to go back
```

The next screen (below) gives you detailed instructions on how to navigate through this law library's computer system. Take note that when you are ready to leave this site, type **q** to quit.

To begin, type **1** (that's the number one) or press **<Enter>**.

```
INSTRUCTIONS:
*Press "left arrow" to Return to the Previous Screen
*Press "down arrow" to move to next selection
*Press "ENTER" on your menu selection
*DO NOT press "esc".  It won't work.
*IF YOU WANT A DOCUMENT THAT YOU ARE VIEWING SENT TO
YOU BY EMAIL,  press "P" while viewing it
*TO CHANGE MENU OPTIONS (want menu selections NUMBERED?),
  press O (options) and follow menu


        [1]Press Enter to Begin

        [2]Leave a comment for SYSOP
         -Mark Folmsbee (zzfolm@acc.wuacc.edu)


        [3]Exit



Commands: Use arrow keys to move, '?' for help, 'q' to quit, '<-' to go back
```

Next, you are presented with a number of subjects from which to select, including an excellent collection of lawyer jokes under number 12. But for the moment, you will follow the directions of your friend and choose Legal Reference- The Virtual Reference Desk, so type **13 <Enter>**.

```
Press Enter on your selection!  *Use "left arrow to go to previous screen.
*Use "arrow" keys to move around!  Questions?  zzfolm@acc.wuacc.edu
[1]About Washburn Law Library
[2]About Washburn University School of Law
[3]Campus and Other Information Systems (National and Local)
[4]Clinical Legal Education Information System (AALS)
[5]Directories-Email/Phone (national and local)
[6]Federal Government Information
[7]Foreign Law and United Nations Materials
[8]Holocaust Information System
[9]Information Network of Kansas (INK)-Password Needed
[10]Law Library Catalogs
[11]Law Library Related Files that may be sent to you by Email
[12]Lawyer Jokes
[13]Legal Reference- The Virtual Reference Desk
[14]Legal Writing and Research Info Sys (TULSA)
[15]Oil and Gas Law Information System
[16]Other Law Systems (Gophers/Hytelnet/WWW/WAIS/Freenet/Usenet/FTP Sites)
[17]Request Washlaw Service?
[18]Search Internet
[19]Telejurist
[20]U.S. Law
-- press space for next page --
```

You are looking for the menu choice Business/Banking Reference Notes. . .

```
(p1 of 5)

THE "VIRTUAL" LAW LIBRARY REFERENCE DESK

_____

  * [1]Washburn University School of Law Library Brochure
  * [2]Library Staff Directory
  * [3]Library Hours
  * [4]Reference Liaison
  * [5]Holiday Tips & Trivia

GATT NEWS
  * [6]General Agreement on Tariffs and Trade

PROFESSORS' CHOICE
  * [7]WEATHER News
  * [8]Holt's Stock Market Report
-- press space for next page --
```

. . .which is not on the screen, so hit the **space bar** to see the next page of options . . .

and the following screen appears, but still no Business/Banking Reference Notes. So hit the **space bar** again to go to the next screen. . .

```
(p2 of 5)
  * [9]Current Foreign Exchange Rates
  * [10]TIME and TRAVEL around the WORLD
  * [11]SUPREME COURT DECISIONS by Date
  * [12]Cornell University's SUPREME COURT DECISION MENU
  * [13]Schedules for CLASSROOM TVs
  * [14]Legal Directories on the Net
  * [15]Chronicle of Higher Education Newsletter
  * [16]LISTSERVS & SUBJECTS / WASHBURN University School of Law
  * [17]LEGAL RESEARCH GUIDES / WASHBURN University School of Law
  * [18]REFERENCE Corner
  * [19]Internet Academic Resources by Subject
  * [20]Historic DOCUMENTS and SPEECHES and BOOKS
  * [21]DECEMBER BOOKS OF THE MONTH: "A Christmas Carol" & "A Cricket
    on the Hearth"
DAILY NEWS
  * [22]Updated News Files
NATIONAL NEWS
  * [23]Proclamation: DECEMBER is DRUNK DRIVING PREVENTION MONTH
  * [24]Current News of National Interest, Speeches, Announcements,
    etc.
-- press space for next page --
```

. . . and the next

```
(p3 of 5)
 ELECTION 1994
  * [25]ELECTION RESULTS, Speeches, Contracts, & Propositions
 LAWS & DOCUMENTS IN THE NEWS
  * [26]Laws, Bills, Bill Signings, etc.
NEWS SOURCES ON THE NET
  * [27]NEWS Lover's NEWS Sources
POLITICAL REFERENCE
  * [28]Elections, Political Gophers, Media Schedules
GOVERNMENT REFERENCE
  * [29]Government Documents, Issues, Access, etc.
  * [30]VERY NEW!!! Welcome to the White House WWW
  * [31]CIA's New WWW!!
INTERNATIONAL REFERENCE
  * [32]International, Foreign, United Nations, etc.
```

. . .till at last we find our heading Business/Banking Reference Notes and
see that number 34 is the link to business information and sources. So
type that number and hit **<Enter>**.

```
                              (p4 of 5)
  * [33]Court Information; Supreme Ct. Decisions; Biographies; CALI
 BUSINESS/BANKING REFERENCE NOTES
  * [34]Business Information and Sources
 INTERNET REFERENCE NEWS
  * [35]Washburn Law LISTSERVS; Gophers; Legal Lists; EDUPAGE;
WUINFO
 MEDIA REFERENCE NOTES
  * [36]Cable Television, Multi-Media, Policies
 GENERAL REFERENCE SOURCES
  * [37]New and Traditional Reference Sources on the Net
 NATIONAL INFORMATION INFRASTRUCTION (NII)
  * [38]Information Infrastructure Gopher and Documents
 FOR LIBRARIANS ONLY
  * [39]BOOKS, Food, Music, and OTTKUS (other things that keep us sane)
  * [40]Lissa's Stuff

-- press space for next page --
follow link number: 34
```

```
                Lynx File Converted to HTML (p1 of 2)
***************************************************************
            THE "VIRTUAL" LAW LIBRARY REFERENCE DESK
            Washburn University School of Law Library
                      Reference Department
                      zzholz@acc.wuacc.edu
***************************************************************
NEWS OF LAW AND BUSINESS
 * [1]President Signing Small Business Reauthorization Act
 * [2]Business in the Law
 * [3]Aerospace Business Development Center WWW
 * [4]EDUPAGE Newsletter
FINANCE
 * [5]Exchanges and Stock Markets
 * [6]Financenet WWW
 * [7]The Chicago Mercantile Exchange
 * [8]Koblas Currency Converter
 * [9]The Accounting Network


follow link number: 1
```

At this point, you see another list of options. To read about the President's signing of the Small Business Reauthorization Act, type **1 <Enter>**.

```
                                              (p1 of 3)
                     THE WHITE HOUSE
                 Office of the Press Secretary
  _____

  For Immediate Release                     October 22, 1994


  STATEMENT BY PRESIDENT CLINTON ON SIGNING OF THE SMALL
                BUSINESS REAUTHORIZATION ACT

      Today I am pleased to sign S. 2060, the "Small Business
  Administration Reauthorization and Amendments Act of 1994."  This Act
  will reauthorize programs of the Small Business Administration (SBA) for
  fiscal years 1995 through 1997, make meaningful program revisions, and
  authorize important new initiatives.  By doing so, the Congress and my
  Administration are carrying out the plans we began in 1993 to make the
  SBA a leaner, more efficient, more effective organization that is
  focused on meeting the needs of all small businesses.
  -- press space for next page --
```

The full text of the press release on the signing of this bill appears (above). At the top of the screen is a parenthetical note that points out this is the first of 3 pages. If you want to save this information, use your local software to download or print this press release page by page. How you download or print will vary depending upon the software you are using to connect to the Internet.

```
(p1 of 3)


                    THE WHITE HOUSE

           Office of the Press Secretary
_____

For Immediate Release            October 22, 1994

  STATEMENT BY PRESIDENT CLINTON ON SIGNING OF THE SMALL
             BUSINESS REAUTHORIZATION ACT
     Today I am pleased to sign S. 2060, the "Small Business
Administration Reauthorization and Amendments Act of 1994."  This Act
will reauthorize programs of the Small Business Administration (SBA) for
fiscal years 1995 through 1997, make meaningful program revisions, and
authorize important new initiatives.  By doing so, the Congress and my
Administration are carrying out the plans we began in 1993 to make the
SBA a leaner, more efficient, more effective organization that is
focused on meeting the needs of all small businesses.
Are you sure you want to quit? [Y]
```

To leave the Washburn Law Library connection, follow the directions that you were given when you first logged in: type **q <Enter>**. Then confirm that you really want to quit by typing **y**, as above.

```
       Thank you for using Lynx Ver. 2.0.11
         (c)1993 University of Kansas
       Lou Montulli (montulli@ukanaix.cc.ukans.edu)
Connection closed by foreign host.
haas 52 ~>
```

You are now disconnected from the Washburn Law School computer and have returned to your local computer connection.

Review

You have used the Telnet command and the appropriate Internet addresses to connect to the Library of Congress and to the Washburn Law School. In both cases, you had to have previously acquired the required login command to complete the connection. You saw how the Telnet connection allows you to operate the systems remotely and how each location uses different methods for navigating and obtaining information.

At this point, you may want to go back to the "Best Bets for Exploration" list and pick some of the Telnet addresses to explore on your own.

MODULE *4* : FTP

Basic facts about FTP

FTP commands

Using FTP to retrieve software

    Example: Retrieving Mosaic software

Using Archie to locate information by subject

    Example: Search for information about NAFTA

Review

FTP (File Transfer Protocol)

- Copies files to your computer
- Public files available via anonymous FTP

BASIC FACTS ABOUT FTP

File Transfer Protocol, or FTP, enables you to retrieve computer files from remote networks. This is an excellent method for quickly transferring large software programs or statistical files. It is particularly useful for downloading Internet programs such as Gopher, Veronica, and Mosaic.

To access files located in a remote computer, you usually need to be an authorized user. However, thousands of sites around the world allow external users to connect to their network and copy files stored in particular directories established for public use, without having prior authorization.

When connected, you are often first asked for a user name, to which you reply **anonymous** (typed in lower case). Then, when asked for a password, type your email address. You are then able to copy files as a "guest." The key word here is "guest": keep in mind that as a guest you must follow any restrictions that are placed on you by the host. Try to avoid tying up the host computer during peak-use periods, when you would be adding to its already heavy traffic.

FTP Commands

- ftp [or] open <machine address>
  Opens connection
- ls Lists files and subdirectories in current directory
- dir Similar to "ls" but shows more detail
- cd <directory name> Changes directory
- get <filename> Transfers remote file
- get <filename> |more
  Displays file without transferring

FTP COMMANDS

Above are the basic commands used to navigate using FTP. They are primarily Unix commands that allow you to look at directories, change directories, view README files, and transfer target files back to your computer. Unix commands are "case sensitive"; that is, you must type file and directory names exactly as they appear, making sure to use uppercase (capital) letters and lowercase letters as indicated.

When transferring a remote file to your computer, you may want to change the name of the file to something that is more meaningful to you. Do this by appending your new file name after the remote file name. For example:

get <remote filename> <local filename>

Caution: Be sure you choose a name that does not already exist in your local directory or the new file will completely replace your old one!

If you want to check out a file before you transfer it to be sure it is what you expected, use the **get** command with **|more**. (The vertical line you see before "more" is called a "pipe"; on your keyboard it looks like a colon made with vertical lines instead of dots.) This command transfers the file to your screen, not to your storage disk. Sometimes it is difficult to tell which directories or files are the ones you want, so an important type of file to look at in this way is a README file. README files are created to explain how information is arranged, and reading these files can help you determine which directories and files to transfer. To view a README file, type **get README |more**.

More FTP Commands

- binary   Changes transfer mode from text (ASCII)
- cdup   Changes directory to "parent" directory
- help   Lists FTP commands available on the remote host
- bye [or] quit   Logs out of remote computer

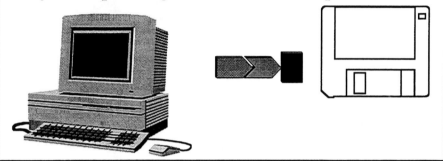

Some files are in binary form and to transfer them you must type the command **binary**. You can usually tell from the extension of the file name whether the file is in binary form or text form. For example, file names ending with these extensions are normally binary: .arc, .com, .exe, .tar, .wp, .z, and .zip.

The command **cdup** is a shortcut to reach the "parent" directory, which is the next directory "up" in the hierarchy.

To exit from your FTP session, type either **quit** or **bye <Enter>.**

USING FTP TO RETRIEVE SOFTWARE

FTP operations cause the heaviest traffic on the Internet as measured by amount of data transmitted. That is because FTP is ideal for moving large files. Often you are obtaining software such as Mosaic or Gopher that are used as application programs on your computer. The examples in this lesson show you how to explore a software archive when you already know where the files exist, but you do not know the exact directory and file names.

The screen below shows the procedure used to logon to a site at UC Berkeley, where you will find software that is used for running Mosaic on the Internet. You already know where the software is located, so type

ftp tuna.berkeley.edu

to logon to the computer that has the software.

When prompted for a name, type

anonymous \<Enter\>

Many systems throughout the world allow guests to logon as "anonymous" users. Your remote host gives information about using this system.

```
Retrieving Mosaic Software via FTP


library% ftp tuna.berkeley.edu
Connected to tuna.berkeley.edu.
220 tuna.Berkeley.EDU FTP server (Version wu-2.1c(1) Mon Sep 27 17:09:52 PDT 199
3) ready.
Name (tuna.berkeley.edu:gpeete): anonymous
331 Guest login ok, send your complete e-mail address as password.
Password:
230-
230- If your FTP client crashes or hangs shortly after login, or the
230- messages are garbled, please try using a dash (-) as the first
230- character of your password.  This will turn off the informational
230- messages that may be confusing your FTP client.
230-
230- Welcome to the WSSG anonymous ftp file server.  If you have any
230- questions or problems with this service, please send email to
230- drmicro@garnet or call our consulting office, 2-8899.
230-
230 Guest login ok, access restrictions apply.
ftp>
```

Next you want to view the file names on this server, so type

ls -l [Caution: That's *lowercase LS space minus-sign lowercase L*]

to get a long list of files.

```
ftp> ls -l
200 PORT command successful.
150 Opening ASCII mode data connection for /bin/ls.
total 4
d--x--x--x    2    0      0     512    Jul 14  1992    bin
drwxr-x--     2    7644   76    512    Aug 23 22:58   mmxp
d--x--x--x    2    0      1     512    Jul 14  1992    msgs
drwxrwxr-x    8    7644   0     512    Mar 8  1994    pub
226 Transfer complete.
remote: -l
251 bytes received in 0.063 seconds (3.9 Kbytes/s)
ftp>
```

The remote host responds with a list of file and directory options. The first column in this list uses codes to tell you whether the entry is a directory (starts with a *d*) and whether you have permission to read the files or write to (change) them. The column with "512" in it gives you the sizes of the files, followed by the dates when the files were created or updated. Last comes the directory or file name.

You decide to try the "pub" directory, so you <u>c</u>hange <u>d</u>irectory to the "pub" directory by typing **cd pub**, as shown below. You then get a brief message about what is contained in this location.

```
ftp> cd pub
250-
250-This is the WSSG anonymous ftp "pub" directory.
250-Each of the directories here contains stuff for
250-the named computer or product.
250-
250 CWD command successful.
ftp>
-rw-r--r--  1 ftpadmin   266688 Jul 18 18:09 wmos20a5.zip
```

Now type **dir <Enter>**, which gives similar information as the "ls -l" command.

```
ftp> dir
200 PORT command successful.
150 Opening ASCII mode data connection for /bin/ls.
total 9
-r--r--r--   1 7644      0          128 Jul 14 1992 .message
drwxr-xr-x  21 7644      0          512 Aug  6 01:49 dos-win
-rw-r--r--   1 7644     20          223 Feb 17 1994 ibmpc-use.dos-
win.instead
-rw-r--r--   1 7644     20          426 Mar  3 1994 mac-use.cornucopia.instea
d
drwxr-xr-x   3 7644      0          512 Sep  6 22:46 micronet
drwxr-xr-x   8 7644      0          512 Jun 25 02:16 netware
drwxr-xr-x   3 7644      0          512 Aug 18 1993 src
drwxr-xr-x   6 7644      0          512 Feb  4 1994 unix
drwxr-xr-x   2 2042      0          512 Sep 23 1992 whs
226 Transfer complete.
613 bytes received in 0.14 seconds (4.4 Kbytes/s)
ftp>
```

Since you are interested in DOS with Windows, type **cd dos-win <Enter>**, as shown below, to get into that directory. Then type **ls -l** to obtain a menu of files in this directory. You can see that there is a directory named "mosaic," so type **cd mosaic <Enter>** to enter that directory.

```
613 bytes received in 0.14 seconds (4.4 Kbytes/s)
ftp> cd dos-win
250-The pub/dos-win directory contains various DOS and Windows programs
250-
250 CWD command successful.
ftp> ls -l
200 PORT command successful.
150 Opening ASCII mode data connection for /bin/ls.
total 19
drwxr-xr-x   2 7644     20          512 Oct  8 1993 archie
drwxr-xr-x   4 7644      0          512 Aug  7 18:58 kermit
drwxr-xr-x   5 7644     20          512 Aug 24 18:47 lanworkplace
drwxr-xr-x   4 7644     20          512 Aug 25 03:40 mcgill
drwxr-xr-x   2 7644      0         1024 Jul  7 17:30 misc
drwxr-xr-x   6 7644     20          512 Jul 21 22:09 mosaic
drwxr-xr-x   6 7644      0          512 Aug  8 22:17 network
drwxr-xr-x   4 7644      0          512 Aug 25 23:22 windows
drwxrwxr-x   2 7644     20          512 Mar 17 18:52 www
226 Transfer complete.
remote: -l
1221 bytes received in 0.52 seconds (2.3 Kbytes/s)
ftp>cd mosaic
```

Now type **ls -l<Enter>** to display a list of the files in the directory "mosaic."

```
ftp> ls -l
200 PORT command successful.
150 Opening ASCII mode data connection for /bin/ls.
total 5
drwxrwxr-x  2 7644    20        512 Jun 16 16:51 disk1
drwxrwxr-x  2 7644    20        512 Jul 21 22:09 fonts
-rw-rw-r--  1 7644    20        584 Jun 16 17:18 install.ucb
drwxrwxr-x  2 7644    20        512 Jun  4 22:21 misc
drwxrwxr-x  3 7644    20        512 Jun 16 16:44 old
226 Transfer complete.
remote: -l
322 bytes received in 0.063 seconds (5 Kbytes/s)
ftp>
```

Notice the file name "install.ucb." You wisely decide to read this file for instructions on how to install the program. To read this file one screen at a time, type **get install.ucb |more<Enter>,** as shown below. This is a Unix command that displays text files to your screen one page at a time without transferring the file to your computer.

```
ftp> ls -l
200 PORT command successful.
150 Opening ASCII mode data connection for /bin/ls.
total 5
drwxrwxr-x  2 7644    20        512 Jun 16 16:51 disk1
drwxrwxr-x  2 7644    20        512 Jul 21 22:09 fonts
-rw-rw-r--  1 7644   20        584 Jun 16 17:18 install.ucb
drwxrwxr-x  2 7644    20        512 Jun  4 22:21 misc
drwxrwxr-x  3 7644    20        512 Jun 16 16:44 old
226 Transfer complete.
remote: -l
322 bytes received in 0.063 seconds (5 Kbytes/s)
ftp>get install.ucb |more
```

This text file tells you what files to copy to obtain the software necessary to run Mosaic and that those files are in the directory "disk1."

```
200 PORT command successful.
Installation Procedures for Mosaic:
 1) FTP the files in the directory disk1 to a formatted BLANK diskette.
   Make sure you use the ftp BINARY option.
    You should have the following files:
   EZGRP   EXE
   INSTALL  EXE
   INSTALL  OLB
   MOSAIC2A LZH
   VIEWERS  LZH
   EZILOGO  TXT
   MOS0001
   MOSAIC  INI
   README  DOC
   README  UCB
   EZI    CFG
2) Exit Windows
3) A:
4) INSTALL
5) Start Windows
--More--
drwxr-sr-x  2 ftpadmin ftp        512 Dec 22  1993 gopher
```

Change to the disk1 directory by typing **cd disk1< Enter>.**

```
ftp> cd disk1
250 CWD command successful.
ftp>
```

Now that you are in the directory where the necessary files are located, you can begin transferring the software for Mosaic by using the "get" command. For example, when you type **get install.exe<Enter >**, the install.exe file will be transferred back to your home computer.

```
ftp>    get    install.exe
200     PORT    command    successful.
150     Opening    ASCII    mode    data    connection    for    install.exe    (69780    bytes).
226     Transfer    complete.
local:    install.exe    remote:    install.exe
70426    bytes    received    in    0.93    seconds    (74    Kbytes/s)
ftp>
```

A shortcut that will save you the trouble of *GET*ting each file separately is the "mget" command, which transfers multiple files. Instead of typing "get <filename>", type

mget * <Enter>

As each file in the directory is retrieved, you will be asked whether you wish to transfer that file--to which you answer yes or no.

Caution: When downloading large files or large numbers of files, make sure you have enough room in your computer to store them. Before issuing the "get" command, type **ls -l<Enter>** to check the size of the files you will transfer.

If you had known the directory and file names you needed ahead of time, you could have gone directly to them by typing the appropriate path when you first logged in: /pub/dos-win/mosaic/disk1. Often this information is provided in a resource guide, in a periodical article, from doing an Archie search (a program that searches the Internet for files by name), or in some other source.

To end your FTP session, type **quit<Enter>** and you are returned to your home computer.

```
ftp> quit
221 Goodbye.
library%
150 Opening ASCII mode data connection for /bin/ls.
tot
```

Use Archie
to Find Locations and Files

- Provides a kind of subject approach
- Easy to use
- Responds with addresses and directories

ARCHIE

Archie is a search program that can help you locate information on a certain topic. To use Archie (often written with the initial letter as a lowercase *a),* you must be connected to a computer that is running the Archie software.

Archie searches are predicated on the premise that the names given to directories and files reflect the subject matter contained in the files. Archie searches for a match between your search term and that same term in its index of directory and file names. Because Archie indexes are not comprised of a controlled vocabulary of subject terms, the results are often not very precise and can produce some unwanted results.

SEARCH FOR INFORMATION ABOUT NAFTA

You have a subject in mind but don't know where on the Internet there is information about it. You hope Archie can help. In the example below, you will connect to a server that is operating archie software.

In this case, you want to find files containing information about the North America Free Trade Agreement, NAFTA. At the prompt (or command line), in this case "haas 52~>", type the command **archie nafta <Enter>**, as shown below.

```
                    SAMPLE ARCHIE SEARCH


haas 52 ~> archie nafta
Host sunsite.unc.edu
     Location: /pub/academic/economics/sci.econ.research/NAFTA
          FILE -rw-r--r--    23611  Nov 16 1993  nafta
     Location: /pub/academic/political-science
       DIRECTORY drwxrwxrwx      512  Feb 27 18:38  nafta
     Location: /pub/academic/political-science/nafta/full-text
       DIRECTORY drwxrwxr-x      512  Feb 24 02:02  nafta
```

When the search is completed, you find that there are numerous sites that contain information on NAFTA. Looking at just the first screen of responses, note that the address of one host computer that has NAFTA information is sunsite.unc.edu, a computer located at the University of North Carolina.

Next, notice the directories where the NAFTA files are located: "Location: /pub/academic/economics/sci.econ.research/NAFTA". In some cases, you can tell what is in the file by the name given to it, but often it is not clear.

The notation "FILE -rw-r--r--" tells you that the creator of this file has permission to read (r) and write (w) to this file, while all others, including you, have permission only to read the file.

The notation "23611 Nov 16 1993" tells you the size of the file and the date it was created.

Next, you copy the address and directory information and perform a file transfer by issuing the following commands:

ftp sunsite.unc.edu<Enter>

cd pub/academic/economics/sci.econ.research<Enter>

get nafta<Enter>

q<Enter>

Review

You now know the primary commands needed to reach out to a remote site, scan directory and file names until you recognize the file you want, and copy it to your computer, checking to be sure you have the disk space for it. You have transferred software comprised of many files, which you accomplished efficiently with one shortcut command. You also looked for material on a subject, and when you found it, performed a file transfer.

Now that you have completed the FTP module, put what you learned to use: check out an FTP site of interest to you listed in the "Best Bets for Exploration" section at the front of this book and go through the steps of transferring a file. FTP is one of the more difficult tools to use because of its command structure, so you may want to keep handy the "Quick Guide" in the Ready Reference Guides for a review of FTP commands.

MODULE *5* : Gopher

Basic facts about Gophers

Gopher commands

Finding business-related statistics

     Example: UC Berkeley's Library Gopher
                 ↓
                Research Databases and Resources
                 ↓
                Economic Indicators and Data
                 ↓
                Economic Bulletin Board (UMich)
                 ↓
                Current Business Statistics
                 ↓
                Labor Force, Employment Earnings

Making a bookmark

Mailing a file to yourself

Using Veronica to find the Consumer Price Index

     Example: UC Berkeley's Library Gopher

                Veronica server at the University of Pisa
                 ↓
                Consumer Price Index
                 ↓

Review

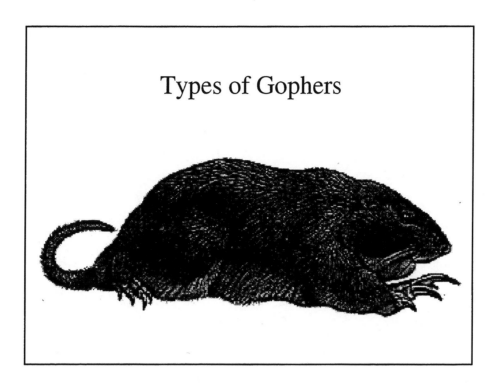

Types of Gophers

A gopher is an animal that ruins your lawn and garden. It can make your life miserable. It also is a front-end program (software used to run other programs) that can make life on the Internet much more enjoyable.

Gophers

- Connect to a Gopher server to use
- Use standard menu commands

BASIC FACTS ABOUT GOPHERS

Developed at the University of Minnesota, Gophers allow you to use a standard menu format to navigate through the Internet. In many ways they combine the functions of email, Telnet, and FTP into one package that allows the user to navigate easily through the Net without requiring the use of line commands. You can login to a remote location, search a database, and send the information back to your email address.

If your local network does not provide a Gopher server, you can telnet to a server and login as a guest.

For the person interested in business-related resources, a number of Internet locations have been "gopherized," that is, many local servers have set up Gopher servers with pointers that automatically log you in to the desired database. In this workshop, you will use various "gopherized" information sources as examples.

Gopher Commands

- ?: Gives online help and describes commands
- q : Quits with prompt
- Q : Quits unconditionally
- = : Displays technical information about the location of current menu selection
- o: Opens a new Gopher server
- O: Changes options
- / : Searches for an item in the menu
- n: Finds next occurrence of search item

GOPHER COMMANDS

A Gopher server allows you to use standard commands. These commands are "case sensitive," which means that you must pay attention to using uppercase and lowercase letters as specified because they have different meanings.

Here are some of the basic Gopher commands:

•A question mark gives you a list of Gopher commands and describes what these commands do.

•A lowercase "q" logs you out after asking you whether you want to quit.

•An uppercase "Q" logs you out of the Gopher session without asking.

•An equal sign (=) tells you the IP address for the file you are looking at.

•A lowercase "o" connects you to another Gopher server directly.

•An uppercase "O" allows you to change options.

•A slash (/) opens up a search box in which you can type a search word or string for finding key words in menus or text.

•A lowercase "n" allows you to find the next occurrence of the word or phrase.

See the "Quick Guide" in the Ready Reference Guides section for more commands.

FINDING BUSINESS-RELATED STATISTICS

With these few commands, you are ready to go step by step through a sample search to explore business-related statistics using a Gopher server at UC Berkeley.

At your Unix prompt, use telnet to get into the Gopher server by typing

telnet infolib.berkeley.edu <Enter>.

```
                  Connecting to UC Berkeley's Library Gopher




              library> telnet infolib.lib.berkeley.edu
              Trying 128.32.224.55 ...
              Connected to infolib.berkeley.edu.
              Escape character is '^]'.


              OSF/1 (infolib.lib.berkeley.edu) (ttyqc)

              login: guest
              TERM = (vt100)
```

Note that once the connection is made, the phrase "Escape character is '^]'." appears. This statement tells us that if you want to stop a process, you press the **Control** key (signified by ^) and the **right bracket** key (]) at the same time.

When prompted for "login," type **guest <Enter>**. Many Gopher servers allow outside unauthorized users to login.

Since the terminal emulation is vt100, simply hit **<Enter>** to accept this option. You may type in other terminal types if necessary to match the communications software you are using.

```
                    SELECTION MENU
             -------------------------------


         1)  Gopher

         2)  Exit


     Please select your choice by Number: 1
```

When connected, you get this screen. Since you want to use the Gopher
program, type 1 **<Enter>**.

```
Internet Gopher Information Client v2.0.14

            InfoLib - The UC Berkeley Library Gopher

--> 1. About InfoLib: The UC Berkeley Library Gopher/
    2. About the Libraries (Hours, News, Instruction, Services, etc.)/
    3. GLADIS Online Catalog (most UCB libraries) <TEL>
    4. MELVYL (tm) UC 9-Campus System <TEL>
    5. Electronic Journals, Books, Indexes, and Other Sources/
    6. Research Databases and Resources by Subject/
    7. New in the UC Berkeley Libraries/
    8. InfoCal (Class Schedule, Campus Phonebook, etc.)/
    9. Other Library Catalogs/
    10. Other Gophers (Campus and World-Wide)/
    11. Search Gopherspace using Veronica/
    12. Search titles in this Gopher  <?>
Press ? for Help, q to Quit                    Page: 1/1
```

You now are presented with a number of options. No matter what Gopher you login to, the opening menu will be a menu of choices like the one shown on this screen. Gopher menus will access a variety of programs types. This one, for example, leads you to information files, interactive library catalogs and journal indexes, and other Gophers. To choose an option, type a menu number and hit **<Enter>**.

At the bottom of the screen are cues: to see a list of Gopher commands in the quick Gopher guide, type **?**. To quit, you would type **q**. Each screen is referred to as a "page," as in "Page: 1/1." You would see a similar line of commands on any Gopher that you logged in to.

Notice that at the end of some lines "<TEL>" appears. This abbreviation alerts you that selecting these options will start a Telnet session. The "<?>" notation at the end of menu option 12 indicates that selecting this option will result in a search.

Type **6<Enter>** to go into a list of choices of research databases and resources by subject.

The next menu gives you a list of different subjects from which to select.

```
Internet Gopher Information Client 2.0 pl10

             Research Databases and Resources by Subject
 --> 1.  Folio & Socrates - Stanford Online System and Catalog (UCB Only)/
     2.  Anthropology/
     3.  Architecture/
     4.  Arts/
     5.  Astronomy/
     6.  Biological Sciences/
     7.  Business/
     8.  Chemistry and Chemical Engineering/
     9.  Computer Science/
     10. Earth Sciences/
     11. Economics/
     12. Education/
     13. Engineering/
     14. Environmental Studies/
     15. Ethnic Studies/
     16. General Reference/
     17. General Social Science Resources/
     18. Geography/
Press ? for Help, q to Quit, u to go up a menu          Page: 1/3
```

At the bottom of the screen, you find "Page:1/3," which tells you that there are two more pages of options. To see the next page, just press the **space bar**. To go back one page, type **b**. Also, if you want to go up one menu level, type **u**. These commands are used to navigate Gopher programs throughout the world.

Since you are interested in business-related information, type **7 <Enter>**.

```
Internet Gopher Information Client 2.0 pl10

                    Business
 --> 1. Berkeley Business Guides/
     2. Economic Indicators and Data/
     3. Public Policy/
     4. International Business/
     5. Economics Working Papers/
     6. Links to Other Useful Gophers/
     7. Guides to Internet Resources in Business & Economics/
     8. Miscellaneous Items of Interest/
     9. Business & Economics Selected New Acquisitions Lists/
     10. CD-ROM Indexes in the Business/Economics Library.
     11. Company Reports & Stock Information/
     12. Electronic Journals/
     13. Industry Information/
     14. Management/
Press ? for Help, q to Quit, u to go up a menu          Page: 1/1
```

GETTING TO STATISTICAL INFORMATION

You now see a list of choices that will lead you to a wide range of business-related information. You are interested in statistics, so type **2 <Enter>.**

```
Internet Gopher Information Client 2.0 pl10

               Economic Indicators and Data

  --> 1.  Bureau of Labor Statistics/
       2.  Business & Economics list of statistics available/
       3.  Economic Bulletin Board  (UMich)/
       4.  Federal Reserve Board Data (IMS Server)/
       5.  Gross State Product Tables (US Bur. of Econ. Analysis)/
       6.  Regional Statistics/
       7.  USDA Statistics/




Press ? for Help, q to Quit, u to go up a menu          Page: 1/1
```

After looking over the selections on this page, transport yourself to a computer in Ann Arbor, Michigan, and link into the Economic Bulletin Board at the University of Michigan by typing **3<Enter>**. As indicated in the "Best Bets for Exploration" section, this is an excellent source for economic data.

```
Internet Gopher Information Client 2.0 pl10

                   Economic Bulletin Board  (UMich)

 -->  1.  IMPORTANT!! README!!/
      2.  Best Market Reports/
      3.  Current Business Statistics/
      4.  Defense Conversion Subcommittee (DCS) Info/
      5.  EBB and Agency Information and misc. files/
      6.  Eastern Europe trade leads/
      7.  Economic Indicators/
      8.  Employment Statistics/
      9.  Energy statistics/
     10.  Foreign Assets Control Program/
     11.  Foreign Trade/
     12.  General Information Files/
Press ? for Help, q to Quit, u to go up a menu            Page: 1/2
```

The new screen presents us with a number of new options. Note that the screen looks like those you saw on the UC Berkeley Library's Gopher in that there are several options to pick from and the same directional information appears at the bottom of the page.   Often the resource provider will have a README file such as option #1.   README files provide important information that users are expected to read before entering the database, information such as what is in the database and restrictions on how guest users may use the system. It is a good idea to read these announcements and honor any limitations that are placed on use. For our purposes of the moment, we will skip that step.

Since you are interested in Current Business Statistics series, type **3<Enter>**.

```
Internet Gopher Information Client 2.0 pl10

                    Current Business Statistics
  -->  1.  About the CBS files.
       2.  Description of CBS data files and formats (bsdata.fmt).
       3.  Changes to CBS data and products (bsnews).
       4.  READ.ME file for CBS file changes (9/7/93).
       5.  About DOS Compressed Files (filename.exe).
       6.  All the BSDC Files (bsdc-all.exe).
       7.  All the BSDC.dat files/
       8.  BCI & BS Public Use Data Products.
       9.  Business Statistics Data - Historical (BSDH) Files/
      10.  Business Statistics Revisions 2/94.
      11.  Business Statistics Revisions 3/94.
      12.  CONV-80C.EXE (DOS compressed).
      13.  Conversion program for BS series-Lotus123 documentation.
      14.  Current Business Statistics: All Files (cbs.exe).
      15.  DOS self-extracting file containing worksheet capabilities.
      16.  How to use conv-80c.exe.
      17.  How to use make123.exe.
      18.  How to use select.exe.
  Press ? for Help, q to Quit, u to go up a menu          Page: 1/2
```

To view the menu options for historical business statistics data, type **9<Enter>**. This selection provides you with historical time series that supplement the current statistics.

```
Internet Gopher Information Client 2.0 pl10
            Business Statistics Data - Historical (BSDH) Files
  -->  1.  General Business Indicators (BSDH-01.DAT).
       2.  Commodity Prices (BSDH-02.DAT).
       3.  Construction and Real Estate (BSDH-03.DAT).
       4.  Domestic Trade (BSDH-04.DAT).
       5.  Labor Force, Employment, Earnings (BSDH-05.DAT).
       6.  Finance (BSDH-06.DAT).
       7.  Foreign Trade of the U.S. (BSDH-07.DAT).
       8.  Transportation and Communication (BSDH-08.DAT).
       9.  Chemicals and Allied Products (BSDH-09.DAT).
      10.  Electric Power and Gas (BSDH-10.DAT).
      11.  Food and Kindred Products; Tobacco (BSDH-11.DAT).
      12.  Leather and Products (BSDH-12.DAT).
      13.  Lumber and Products (BSDH-13.DAT).
      14.  Metals and Manufactures (BSDH-14.DAT).
      15.  Petroleum, Coal, and Products (BSDH-15.DAT).
      16.  Pulp, Paper, and Paper Products (BSDH-16.DAT).
      17.  Rubber and Rubber Products (BSDH-17.DAT).
      18.  Stone, Clay, and Glass Products (BSDH-18.DAT).

  Press ? for Help, q to Quit, u to go up a menu          Page: 1/2
```

Now you want to see labor force, employment, and earnings data, so type **5 <Enter>**.

MAKING A BOOKMARK

Or, if you think you will want to return to this site sometime in the future, you can make a bookmark by typing **a<Enter>**.

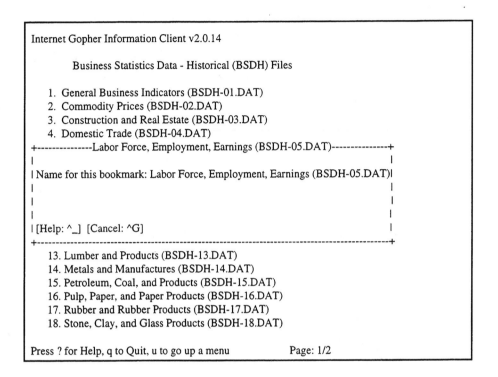

```
Internet Gopher Information Client v2.0.14

         Business Statistics Data - Historical (BSDH) Files

     1. General Business Indicators (BSDH-01.DAT)
     2. Commodity Prices (BSDH-02.DAT)
     3. Construction and Real Estate (BSDH-03.DAT)
     4. Domestic Trade (BSDH-04.DAT)
+---------------Labor Force, Employment, Earnings (BSDH-05.DAT)---------------+
|                                                                            |
| Name for this bookmark: Labor Force, Employment, Earnings (BSDH-05.DAT)|
|                                                                            |
|                                                                            |
|                                                                            |
| [Help: ^_]  [Cancel: ^G]                                                   |
+----------------------------------------------------------------------------+
     13. Lumber and Products (BSDH-13.DAT)
     14. Metals and Manufactures (BSDH-14.DAT)
     15. Petroleum, Coal, and Products (BSDH-15.DAT)
     16. Pulp, Paper, and Paper Products (BSDH-16.DAT)
     17. Rubber and Rubber Products (BSDH-17.DAT)
     18. Stone, Clay, and Glass Products (BSDH-18.DAT)

Press ? for Help, q to Quit, u to go up a menu          Page: 1/2
```

This command will open up a text box like the one on this screen and asks whether you want to accept this name for the bookmark. You can accept it by hitting **<Enter>** or rename the bookmark by editing the text, substituting a name that is more meaningful to you. Now any time you want to return to this source, all you have to do is type **v** when you are in your Gopher server and select the appropriate option from your bookmark menu. You will be brought directly to this menu, thus saving you the trouble of both remembering the path that got you here and keying your way through it.

Bookmark Commands

- v : View bookmark list
- a : Add current item to the bookmark list
- A : Add current directory/search to bookmark list
- d : Delete a bookmark/directory entry

Bookmarks allow you to create your own menu for connecting to the sites on the Internet where you will want to return to in the future. It is like putting a bookmark in a book so you can easily find your place in the future. These bookmark lists are maintained on your home computer and stored in your user file; therefore you must be logged in to the Net through your local computer's Gopher server for this program to work.

•If you type **v**, you are given the list of Internet locations that you have saved.

•To add to the bookmark list either type a lowercase **a** to create an entry linked directly to a particular file, or type an uppercase **A** to make a link to the menu where the item appears.

•To delete a listing from your bookmark menu, type **d**.

MAILING THE FILE TO YOURSELF

Here is the data that you selected. If you want to send the data back to your email address, you can type **m**.

```
Labor Force, Employment, Earnings (BSDH-05.DAT) (1750k)          0%
+-------------------------------------------------------------------------+
         J:\BSHIST\BSDH-05.DAT              FILE LABEL: J:\IDCODES\BSD
C-05.EBB                 (File created 4/ 6/1994)
EM0015   Total noninstitutional pop.: persons 16 years of age & over
                MI194801B194701E199403U940405AVGM0
       ANNUAL   JAN    FEB    MAR    APR    MAY    JUN
   JUL    AUG    SEP    OCT    NOV    DEC    YEAR
   1947  -999999 -999999 -999999 -999999 -999999 -999999 -999999
 -999999 -999999 -999999 -999999 -999999 -999999 1947
   1948  104524. 103994. 104074. 104157. 104217. 104311. 104403.
 104659. 104715. 104807. 104902. 104988. 105071. 1948
   1949  105610. 105147. 105217. 105306. 105381. 105464. 105548.
 105655. 105739. 105828. 105933. 106007. 106104. 1949
   1950  106164. 105730. 105820. 106088. 106006. 106059. 106137.
 106226. 106323. 106341. 106376. 106444. 106436. 1950
   1951  106764. 106492. 106449. 106627. 106635. 106657. 106713.
 106805. 106836. 106901. 106958. 106971. 107134. 1951
   1952  107617. 107206. 107257. 107320. 107391. 107459. 107569.
 107641. 107730. 107817. 107898. 108003. 108093. 1952
   1953  109287. 108884. 108928. 108964. 109086. 109165. 109262.
 109301. 109352. 109471. 109566. 109667. 109782. 1953
+-------------------------------------------------------------------------+
[PageDown: <SPACE>] [Help: ?] [Exit: u]
```

To exit this file, type **u**.

The command **m** will open a text box that asks for the email address where you want to send the information.

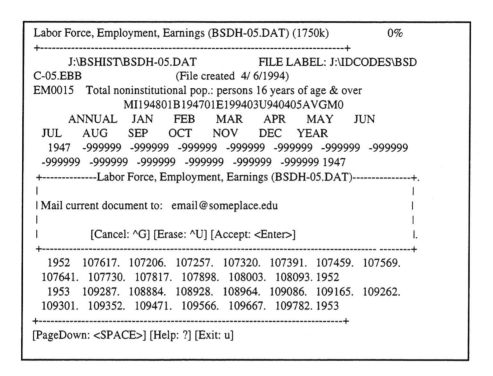

```
Labor Force, Employment, Earnings (BSDH-05.DAT) (1750k)              0%
+----------------------------------------------------------------------+
          J:\BSHIST\BSDH-05.DAT              FILE LABEL: J:\IDCODES\BSD
C-05.EBB                 (File created  4/ 6/1994)
EM0015   Total noninstitutional pop.: persons 16 years of age & over
                 MI194801B194701E199403U940405AVGM0
          ANNUAL   JAN    FEB    MAR    APR    MAY    JUN
  JUL    AUG    SEP    OCT    NOV    DEC    YEAR
   1947  -999999  -999999  -999999  -999999  -999999  -999999  -999999
 -999999  -999999  -999999  -999999  -999999  -999999 1947
 +--------------Labor Force, Employment, Earnings (BSDH-05.DAT)--------------+.
 |                                                                   |
 | Mail current document to:  email@someplace.edu                    |
 |                                                                   |
 |       [Cancel: ^G] [Erase: ^U] [Accept: <Enter>]                  |.
 +----------------------------------------------------------------- --------+
   1952  107617.  107206.  107257.  107320.  107391.  107459.  107569.
 107641.  107730.  107817.  107898.  108003.  108093. 1952
   1953  109287.  108884.  108928.  108964.  109086.  109165.  109262.
 109301.  109352.  109471.  109566.  109667.  109782. 1953
 +---------------------------------------------------------------------+
[PageDown: <SPACE>] [Help: ?] [Exit: u]
```

You would type your complete email address and hit **<Enter>** to send the information back to your mailbox. At the bottom of the box, commands are given for canceling (**Control-G**) or erasing (**Control-U**).

If you want to go back and explore other menu options at Michigan or go back to your original connection at Berkeley, you can back out of the current menu list by typing **u** until you arrive at the desired menu level. If you want to exit from the Gopher session completely, type **q**.

For our purposes, type **g,** so you can return to the menu at UC Berkeley and perform a Veronica search.

VERONICA

- Searches Gopher servers to locate files
- Allows you to connect directly
- Enables you to use an easy or more complicated search strategy

Veronica (Very easy rodent-oriented net-wide index to computerized archives) is a program that searches Gopher systems throughout the world for your search subject. It creates a list of sites that have file titles containing words that match those in your query. Once Veronica locates the sites that meet your needs, you are presented with a list of hits. You can login to a site just by typing the number corrresponding to your choice from that list.

Veronica searches can be very slow. Also, since they are searching through menu text as opposed to subject terms, Veronica searches can often provide leads to sources that do not fit your needs.

```
Internet Gopher Information Client v2.0.14

        InfoLib - The UC Berkeley Library Gopher

   1.  About InfoLib: The UC Berkeley Library Gopher/
   2.  About the Libraries (Hours, News, Instruction, Services, etc.)/
   3.  GLADIS Online Catalog (most UCB libraries)  <TEL>
   4.  MELVYL (tm) UC 9-Campus System <TEL>
   5.  Electronic Journals, Books, Indexes, and Other Sources/
   6.  Research Databases and Resources by Subject/
   7.  New in the UC Berkeley Libraries/
   8.  InfoCal (Class Schedule, Campus Phonebook, etc.)/
   9.  Other Library Catalogs/
   10. Other Gophers (Campus and World-Wide)/
-->  11. Search Gopherspace using Veronica/
   12. Search titles in this Gopher  <?>


Press ? for Help, q to Quit                Page: 1/1
```

SEARCHING FOR THE CONSUMER PRICE INDEX

When you quit your connection at the Economic Bulletin Board at the University of Michigan, you returned to the menu options at UC Berkeley.

Now type **11 <Enter>** to search Gophers around the world for information on the Consumer Price Index, commonly referred to by its initials "CPI."

If you were starting from scratch and not already logged in to the Gopher server, you would type **telnet infolib.berkeley.edu <Enter>** at the Unix prompt.

When prompted for "login", you type **guest <Enter>**.

Hit **<Enter>** to accept the terminal emulation vt100, or type in another terminal type that matches your communications software.

```
Internet Gopher Information Client v2.0.14

                Search Gopherspace using Veronica

    1.  veronica FAQ (from Nevada)
    2.  How to compose veronica queries (from Nevada)
    3.  veronica server at UNINETT/U. of Bergen <?>
--> 4.  veronica server at University of Pisa <?>
    5.  veronica server at University of Koeln <?>
    6.  veronica server at U. of Manitoba <?>
    7.  veronica server at NYSERNet <?>
    8.  Search Gopher Directory Titles at UNINETT/U. of Bergen <?>
    9.  Search Gopher Directory Titles at University of Pisa <?>
    10. Search Gopher Directory Titles at University of Koeln <?>
    11. Search Gopher Directory Titles at U. of Manitoba <?>
    12. Search Gopher Directory Titles at NYSERNet <?>

Press ? for Help, q to Quit, u to go up a menu          Page: 1/1
```

The Gopher menu lists several different Veronica locations to try. One is in the United States, the others are in other countries. The <?> symbol at the end of some of the menu options tells you that picking that selection will begin a search operation. Select the University of Pisa server by typing **4<Enter>** to begin a search.

```
Internet Gopher Information Client v2.0.14

             Search Gopherspace using Veronica

   1.  veronica FAQ (from Nevada)
   2.  How to compose veronica queries (from Nevada)
   3.  veronica server at UNINETT/U. of Bergen <?>
--> 4.  veronica server at University of Pisa <?>
+--------------------veronica server at University of Pisa--------------------+
|                                                                             |
| Words to search for cpi                                                     |
|                                                                             |
|                                                                             |
|                                                                             |
| [Help: ^_]  [Cancel: ^G]                                                    |
+-----------------------------------------------------------------------------+


Press ? for Help, q to Quit, u to go up a menu          Page: 1/1
```

Now a text box opens up where you type your search query: **cpi <Enter>**.
Notice that if you need help, you press the **Control** and **underline** keys
simultaneously. Or to cancel the search, you type **^G** (or **Control key-G)..**

```
Internet Gopher Information Client v2.0.14
              veronica server at University of Pisa: cpi
     1. cp866.cpi
     2. cp866.cpi
     3. CPI - June 1994
     4. Re: CPI - June 1994
     5. cpi_ppi.wk1 <Bin>
     6. LaserWriter: How to Print 21 cpi When Using PCL (3 93)
     7. 6.0369  New Lists: CPI-L; ETHNOHIS (2/63)
     8. Sponsors bill to eliminate tobacco from CPI (11/1/93)
     9. CPI      Characters Per Inch + Clock Per Instruction +
    10. CPI-C    Common Programming Interface for Communications [IBM]
    11. CPI History
    12. CPI Monthly Summary
    13. cpi-1
 --> 14. cpi-2
    15. cpi/
    16. CPI
    17.  Retail sales rise 4th straight month; CPI up 0.4
    18. Prestige Elite 12 cpi de la NEC P5300

Press ? for Help, q to Quit, u to go up a menu          Page: 1/6
```

It can take a long time to conduct such a word search and often the search doesn't work, so your patience is required. The result of this search is six pages of potential sites where information on the CPI resides. Note that in the lower right corner of the screen you are told you are on page 1 of 6 pages.

To see the next page, hit the **space bar**.

```
Internet Gopher Information Client v2.0.14
              veronica server at University of Pisa: cpi
    19. FCR approves tuition caps linked to CPI, enhanced lecturer status
    20. Lower June CPI may augur well for the stockmarket
    21. Lower June CPI may augur well for the stockmarket
    22. cpi.exe-1
    23. cpi.exe-1
    24. LaserWriter: How to Print 21 cpi When Using PCL (3 93)
    25. FCR approves tuition caps linked to CPI, enhanced lecturer status
    26. LaserWriter: How to Print 21 cpi When Using PCL (3 93)
    27. CPI urban consumers by commodity (seasonally adjusted)
    28. CPI urban consumers by area
    29. CPI urban wage earners by commodity
    30. CPI urban wage earners by commodity (seasonally adjusted)
    31. CPI urban wage earners by area
 --> 32. Consumer price index full release (cpi.exe)
    33. xtra.cpi
    34. Communist Party of India (CPI) election campaign video>
    35. Communist Party of India (CPI) election campaign video>
    36. Communist Party of India (CPI) election campaign video>

View item number: 32
```

To look at the Consumer Price Index full release, type **32 <Enter>**.

When you are connected, you see a screen with information about the database. As with the original word search, it often can take some time to get connected and numerous things can go wrong.

```
+-----------------------------------------------------------------------+
| Consumer price index full release (cpi.exe) (81k)            0%       |
| +---------------------------------------------------------------+     |
| FOR TECHNICAL INFORMATION                                            |
| Patrick C. Jackman (202) 606-7000  USDL-94-400                       |
|                          TRANSMISSION OF MATERIAL IN                 |
| CPI Quickline:    (202) 606-6994  THIS RELEASE IS EMBARGOED          |
| FOR CURRENT AND HISTORICAL        UNTIL 8:30 A.M. (EDT)              |
| INFORMATION:      (202) 606-7828  Friday, August 12, 1994            |
| MEDIA CONTACT:    (202) 606-5902                                     |
|                                                                       |
|        CONSUMER PRICE INDEX--JULY 1994                               |
|                                                                       |
|    The Consumer Price Index for All Urban Consumers (CPI-U) rose     |
| 0.3 percent before seasonal adjustment in July to a level of 148.4   |
| (1982-84=100), the Bureau of Labor Statistics of the U.S.            |
| Department of Labor reported today.  For the 12-month period ended   |
| in July, the CPI-U increased 2.8 percent.                            |
|                                                                       |
|    The Consumer Price Index for Urban Wage Earners and Clerical      |
| +---------------------------------------------------------------+     |
| [Help: ?] [Exit: u] [PageDown: Space]                                |
+-----------------------------------------------------------------------+
```

Press the **space bar** to see the next page.

```
+-----------------------------------------------------------------------+
| Consumer price index full release (cpi.exe) (81k)            2%       |
| +---------------------------------------------------------------+     |
| Workers (CPI-W) also increased 0.3 percent in July, prior to         |
| seasonal adjustment.  The July 1994 CPI-W level of 145.8 was 2.6     |
| percent higher than the index in July 1993.                          |
|                                                                       |
| CPI for All Urban Consumers (CPI-U)                                  |
| _____                                 |
|                                                                       |
|    On a seasonally adjusted basis, the CPI-U rose 0.3 percent in     |
| July, the same as in June.  The food and energy indexes, which had   |
| a moderating effect on the CPI-U during the first half of 1994,      |
| increased 0.5 and 1.8 percent, respectively, in July.  Within the    |
| food component, increases in prices for fresh fruits and vegetables  |
| and coffee were partially offset by price declines for meats and     |
| dairy products.  A sharp increase in prices for motor fuels--up 3.8  |
| percent after seasonal adjustment--accounted for nearly 90 percent   |
| of the advance in the energy index.  The  CPI-U excluding food and   |
| energy rose 0.2 percent in July, following increases of 0.3 percent  |
| in each of the preceding 2 months.  A downturn in the index for      |
| apparel and upkeep was responsible for the moderation.               |
| +---------------------------------------------------------------+     |
| [Help: ?] [Exit: u] [PageDown: Space] [PageUp: b]                    |
+-----------------------------------------------------------------------+
```

Again press the **space bar to** get to the next page.

You have now arrived at the data you are seeking.

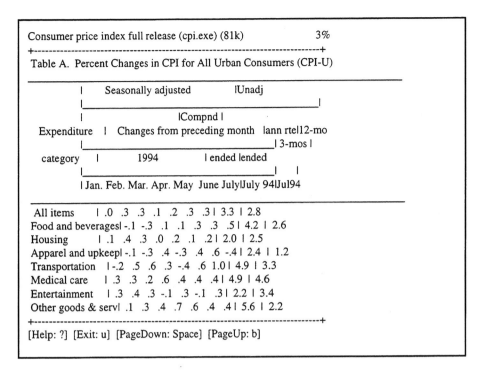

```
+-----------------------------------------------------------------+
| Consumer price index full release (cpi.exe) (81k)          3%   |
| +---------------------------------------------------------+     |
|  Table A.  Percent Changes in CPI for All Urban Consumers (CPI-U) |
|  _____            |
|            |      Seasonally adjusted        |Unadj             |
|            |_____|          |
|            |                    |Compnd |                        |
|  Expenditure  |   Changes from preceding month  |ann rte|12-mo   |
|            |_____| 3-mos |          |
|  category  |          1994          | ended |ended   |   |       |
|            |_____|   |       |
|            | Jan. Feb. Mar. Apr. May  June July|July 94|Jul94    |
|  _____        |
|  All items       | .0  .3  .3  .1  .2  .3  .3| 3.3 | 2.8         |
|  Food and beverages| -.1 -.3  .1  .1  .3  .3  .5| 4.2 | 2.6       |
|  Housing         | .1  .4  .3  .0  .2  .1  .2| 2.0 | 2.5         |
|  Apparel and upkeep| -.1 -.3  .4 -.3  .4  .6 -.4| 2.4 | 1.2       |
|  Transportation  | -.2  .5  .6  .3 -.4  .6 1.0| 4.9 | 3.3        |
|  Medical care    | .3  .3  .2  .6  .4  .4  .4| 4.9 | 4.6         |
|  Entertainment   | .3  .4  .3 -.1  .3 -.1  .3| 2.2 | 3.4         |
|  Other goods & serv| .1  .3  .4  .7  .6  .4  .4| 5.6 | 2.2        |
|  +--------------------------------------------------------+      |
|  [Help: ?]  [Exit: u]  [PageDown: Space]  [PageUp: b]           |
+-----------------------------------------------------------------+
```

If you want to send the information back to your email address, you would type **m**. A text box such as the one in the screen below would open and ask for the address where you want the information sent. After you type in the appropriate email address and hit < **Enter>**, the entire file will be sent to your emailbox.

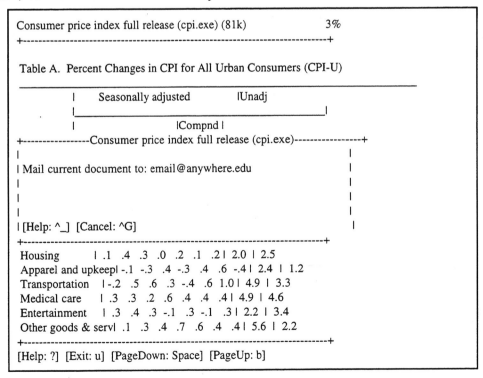

```
+-----------------------------------------------------------------+
| Consumer price index full release (cpi.exe) (81k)          3%   |
| +---------------------------------------------------------+     |
|                                                                 |
|  Table A.  Percent Changes in CPI for All Urban Consumers (CPI-U) |
|  _____            |
|            |      Seasonally adjusted        |Unadj             |
|            |_____|          |
|            |                    |Compnd |                        |
|  +-----------------Consumer price index full release (cpi.exe)-----------------+ |
|  |                                                         |     |
|  | Mail current document to: email@anywhere.edu            |     |
|  |                                                         |     |
|  |                                                         |     |
|  |                                                         |     |
|  | [Help: ^_]  [Cancel: ^G]                                |     |
|  +---------------------------------------------------------+     |
|  Housing         | .1  .4  .3  .0  .2  .1  .2| 2.0 | 2.5         |
|  Apparel and upkeep| -.1 -.3  .4 -.3  .4  .6 -.4| 2.4 | 1.2       |
|  Transportation  | -.2  .5  .6  .3 -.4  .6 1.0| 4.9 | 3.3        |
|  Medical care    | .3  .3  .2  .6  .4  .4  .4| 4.9 | 4.6         |
|  Entertainment   | .3  .4  .3 -.1  .3 -.1  .3| 2.2 | 3.4         |
|  Other goods & serv| .1  .3  .4  .7  .6  .4  .4| 5.6 | 2.2        |
|  +--------------------------------------------------------+      |
|  [Help: ?]  [Exit: u]  [PageDown: Space]  [PageUp: b]           |
+-----------------------------------------------------------------+
```

Also, you can make a bookmark so you can return to this information site in the future by typing **a**. You get a text box with the name of the file that you can use in your bookmark directory; hit **<Enter>** to save the file name as it appears, or edit the file name and hit **<Enter>**.

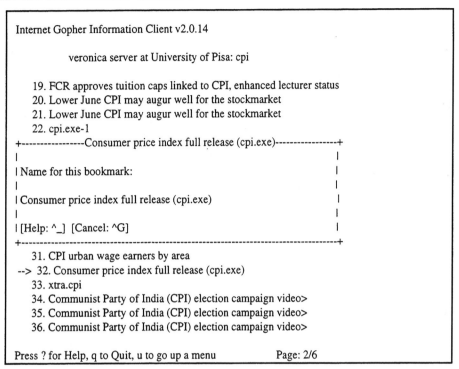

```
Internet Gopher Information Client v2.0.14

        veronica server at University of Pisa: cpi

   19. FCR approves tuition caps linked to CPI, enhanced lecturer status
   20. Lower June CPI may augur well for the stockmarket
   21. Lower June CPI may augur well for the stockmarket
   22. cpi.exe-1
+----------------Consumer price index full release (cpi.exe)----------------+
|                                                                   |
| Name for this bookmark:                                           |
|                                                                   |
| Consumer price index full release (cpi.exe)                       |
|                                                                   |
| [Help: ^_]  [Cancel: ^G]                                          |
+-------------------------------------------------------------------+
   31. CPI urban wage earners by area
-->  32. Consumer price index full release (cpi.exe)
   33. xtra.cpi
   34. Communist Party of India (CPI) election campaign video>
   35. Communist Party of India (CPI) election campaign video>
   36. Communist Party of India (CPI) election campaign video>

Press ? for Help, q to Quit, u to go up a menu          Page: 2/6
```

To quit the search, you type **q**.

Review

You are now an experienced Gopher user. You have used this Internet tool in two situations:

(1) to access information by first going to a Gopher server known to have the type of information you want, and then moving through its layers of menus to get to what you were looking for; and

(2) to search worldwide, using Veronica, for a Gopher server that will guide you to the information you are looking for, choosing one that looks promising, and browsing through it until you find the information that you are seeking.

You have also created bookmarks in your personal directory of Gopher addresses so that you can henceforth return directly to those databases, and you can copy to your emailbox a file you want to save.

To practice more on your own, select one of the Gopher sites you marked in the "Best Bets for Exploration" section at the front of this book and see if you can find information on a topic that interests you.

MODULE *6* : World Wide Web

Basic facts

Mosaic

    The promise

    The problems

Using Yahoo to gather information about mutual funds

    Examples: Markets and investment information

                    Corporate reports

                    Quarterly earnings reports

                    10-K reports

Tips for customizing your Web browser for speed or ease

Review

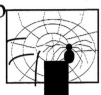

World Wide Web

- Also called The Web, or WWW, or W3
- Uses hypertext to link to related information
  - in the same database
  - in other databases
- You can click on icons and hypertext to access:
  - texts
  - images
  - moving pictures
  - sounds
- Works like Windows and Mac software
- Mosaic: Use it to search W3

BASIC FACTS ABOUT THE WORLD WIDE WEB

The World Wide Web (sometimes called W3, or WWW, or "the Web") is a project started at CERN, the European Laboratory for Particle Physics, located in Geneva, Switzerland. It has grown well beyond being just a project. Sun Microsystems estimated in February 1995 that there were 27,000 Web sites and that this number doubles about every 53 days ("Cyberspace, Crafting Software That Will Let You Build a Business Out There," *Business Week* 27 February 1995, p. 80). The Web uses hypertext (text that is highlighted) to provide information links for the reader. As you will see, these links work like the menu options in Gopher, but they can provide access to still pictures, moving pictures, and audio sources (sometimes referred to as "hypermedia documents") as well as to text. Just the "clicking" of the mouse cursor on a word or phrase in bold print allows you to connect to information on the topic.

Mosaic

There are several software programs that can be used to search W3. They include Mosaic, Netscape and Netcruiser, among others. In this lesson we will demonstrate Mosaic. It is quite popular because it is shareware (available free of charge, as you saw when you transferred Mosaic software to your computer in Module 4, "FTP"); and it has been consistently improved by its creators at the National Center for Supercomputing Applications (NCSA), located at the University of Illinois, Urbana-Champaign. Also, other programs are similar enough for you to be able to transfer what you learn here to other software, even though a particular feature may look different.

Mosaic: Promise

- New programs and hardware
- Local access is expanding
- Large telecommunications providers entering the market
- Wider bandwidths promise faster transfer

Mosaic is still in the testing phase of development. Such early versions usually perform adequately, but occasionally encounter problems and cause Windows programs to display error messages. You have to acquire this software either through FTP from an archive containing the program, such as the University of Illinois (FTP to **ftp.ncsa.uiuc.edu** and directory is /Web/Mosaic/Windows) or by obtaining the necessary disks from some other source, such as a friend. You must install the program on your computer and click on the Mosaic icon to start the program. (Installation instructions are beyond the scope of this book; consult one of the introductory books listed in the "Background Reading" section or the README files that are usually available from the site where you obtained the Mosaic program.)

The Promise

•New commercially produced Web search products such as Netscape are increasing the efficiency of searching the Net, and newer operating systems such as Windows '95 and OS/2's Warp have integrated the necessary connection and viewing software.

•More and more local Internet providers are offering SLIP or PPP connections at relatively low monthly rates.

•Large telecommunications companies are offering high-speed data connections that have speeded up transmission rates and are working on beefing up the ability to carry increasingly larger loads.

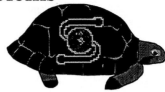

Mosaic: Problems

- Still developing
- Need SLIP or PPP connection
- Very slow response--graphics, sounds, and movies create huge files
- Need fast machine with lots of memory

THE PROBLEMS

•To use Mosaic on the Internet, you must either have a direct connection to the Net or dial in to a server that allows for the SLIP or PPP protocol. More and more research and commercial sites are offering this type of dialin access, but it is still somewhat limited. You also must have viewers loaded in your computer that can read video, audio, and graphics files.

•The huge file size needed to support visuals and sounds (often a megabyte or more) can take minutes to load into your computer even when you have a fast connection and powerful equipment.

> *TIP:* You can speed up access considerably by going into the <u>O</u>ptions pulldown menu and turn off the "Display inline images" feature that automatically displays graphics. Text will be transferred without the accompanying graphics that take so long to display.

•You will need at least a 386 or faster DOS machine with at least 4 megabytes of memory and at least a 9600 baud rate modem with compression capabilities to adequately use Mosaic.

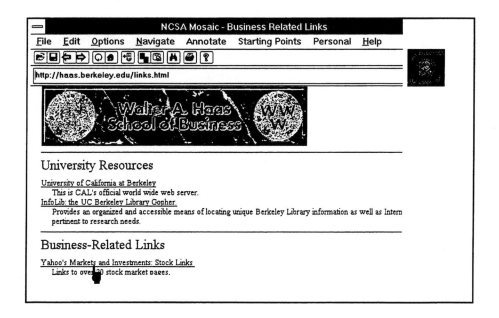

USING YAHOO TO GATHER INFORMATION ABOUT MUTUAL FUNDS

Start off at the homepage of your Web provider. A homepage is the opening screen that provides general information about the site or resource you are "visiting." In any homepage, you will see point-to-and-click icons or "buttons" and highlighted terms that link you to other "pages" of the site or even to other sites. The screen above shows the homepage created at the Haas School of Business at the University of California. To follow this demonstration to the letter, go to the Haas homepage (**http://haas.berkeley.edu/links.htm**). You can configure your computer to use any homepage that you choose. This screen uses Mosaic, which is one method for navigating through the World-Wide Web as well as accessing other sites that are not graphically interfaced, such as Gopher, Telnet, and FTP locations. In addition, Mosaic has the ability to display pictures, show movies, and play sounds.

Note, too, the row of pulldown menu options across the top of the screen, just as in Windows and Macintosh applications. If you click on any of the menu options, you will display submenus that allow you to open and save files, cut and paste, and other operations. The icons below the top row allow you to take shortcuts for executing various operations such as opening a URL file, saving to disk, going back and forth between connections, reloading screens, returning to your homepage, adding a site to your hotlist (adding bookmarks), copying and pasting material, searching for a term, printing , and obtaining help.

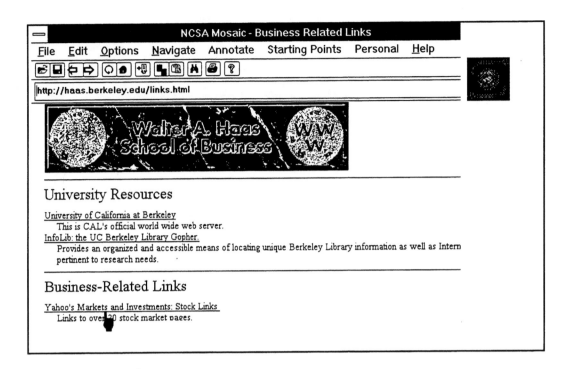

The box below the icons shows to what URL you are connected. If you wanted to go another site on the Net, you could either type in a new address or paste in an address copied from another source, and hit **<Enter>**.

To the far right notice a globe design. While Mosaic performs an operation, the globe rotates. If you ever want to stop an activity such as linking to another Web site, you just click the mouse cursor on the rotating globe and the operation will cease.

Look at the text below the Haas logo and see that certain words are highlighted with underlining (in a color display these terms would be highlighted in a different color than the rest of the text). The highlighted words are hypertext links: when you click the mouse cursor on one of them, you are connected to another file somewhere else within that site or to another site on the Net that provides more information or executes some operation. When the cursor is put on executable hypertext, it changes from an arrow ⇦ to a pointing hand ☝ .

Now click on the phrase "Yahoo's Markets and Investments: Stock Links" under "Business-Related Links"; you will be transported to a Web index at Stanford University. (The Yahoo screens on the following pages were printed with permission.)

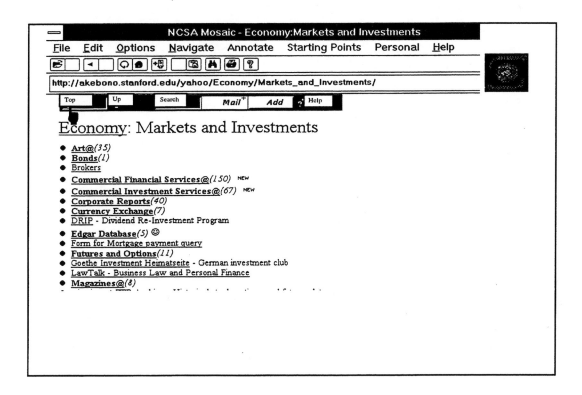

Having clicked on the hypertext link to a submenu in the Yahoo index, a reference to market and investment information appears. Yahoo (Yet Another Hierarchically Officious Oracle) is a powerful index to thousands of resource sites on the Internet. This subject menu has a number of entries on topics you can select--including bonds, brokers, corporate reports, and business law. Clicking on any of these entries would put you into another submenu which would list entries indicated in parentheses.

Looking at the top of the screen below the URL address box, see the various icon buttons. Clicking on the "Top" button takes you to the main menu on Yahoo. The "up arrow" button takes you up one menu level. The "Search" (magnifying glass) button activates a search of menu titles. "Mail" allows you to send comments to the operators of Yahoo. "Add" lets you suggest additions to the index. And "Help" (question mark) gives you instructions for using Yahoo.

Click on the "Top" button to switch to the top level menu.

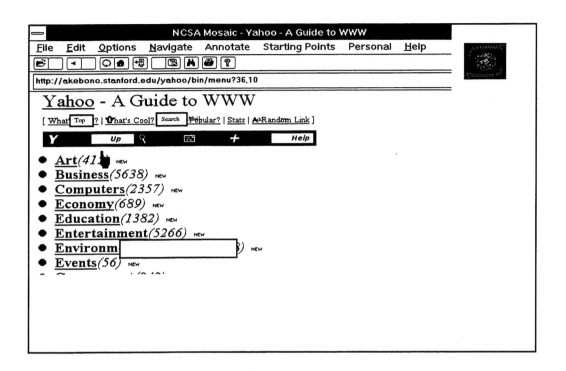

The top level menu at Yahoo is divided into broad subject areas. Yahoo primarily is a guide to HTML resources, but it does contain other types of URLs. The number in parentheses next to each of the subject choices provides the total number of options linked to that category. Note that when this screen was copied that there were 5638 entries for business sources.

Click on "Business." See how the mouse cursor first appears as an arrow and then forms a pointing hand when it points at an Internet link.

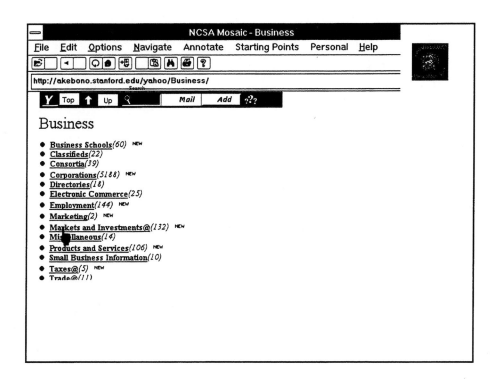

The Business page offers a menu of subtopics. Again, the number in parentheses shows the number of options available under each entry.

Start by clicking on "Markets and Investments."

You now have a number of new choices. Notice that some of the entries have the word *NEW* next to them. This notation indicates that the entry was added within the last three days. The ones with happy faces refer to the sites that the creators of Yahoo feel best cover the presentation or content of the topic indicated.

Click on "Mutual Funds."

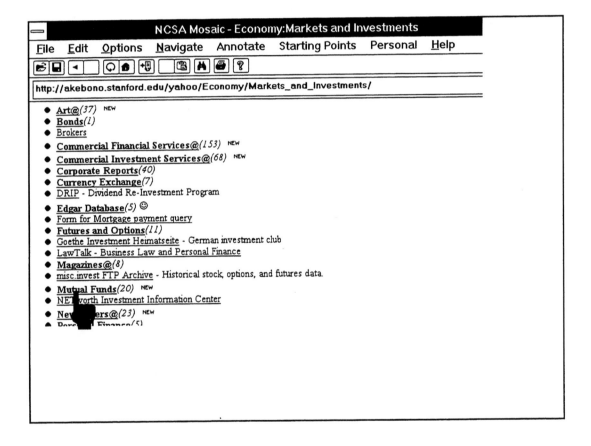

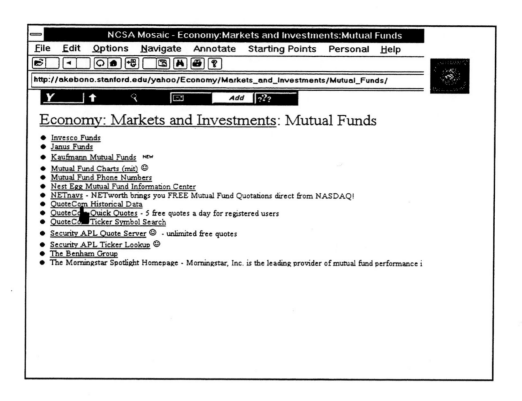

To explore some of the sites listed here, click on "QuoteCom Historical Data."

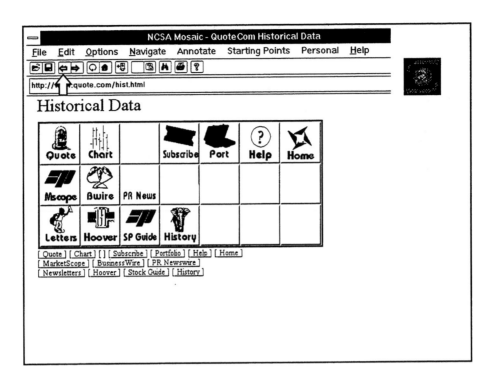

You find that this page is an example of a commercial source that is designed to sell a product. It provides a grid with various information offerings. Stock quotations ("Quote"), Hoover's Handbooks ("Hoover"), and Standard and Poor ("SP Guide") information are some of the options available by clicking on the desired resource. Some of the information is offered free of charge on limited basis to registered users, but most of the information must be bought. The giveaway sources are intended to attract users who will become paying customers once they discover what is available. For instance, historical quotes ("History") are available at $1.95 per file.

To return to the previous menu, click on the left arrow symbol in the icon menu. Notice that the mouse cursor is an arrow now, not a pointing hand, because you are clicking on a menu icon, not a hypertext selection.

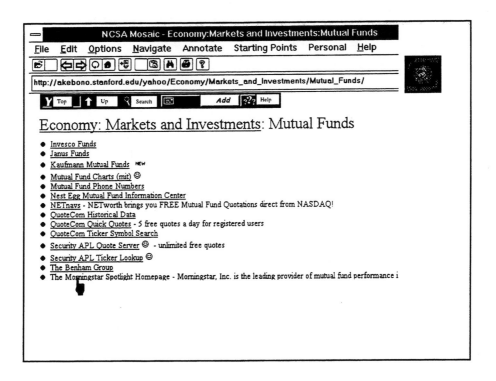

Morningstar, Inc., one of the leading evaluators of mutual fund performance, has a menu entry.

Click on "The Morningstar Spotlight Homepage" to see what this company is offering on the Internet.

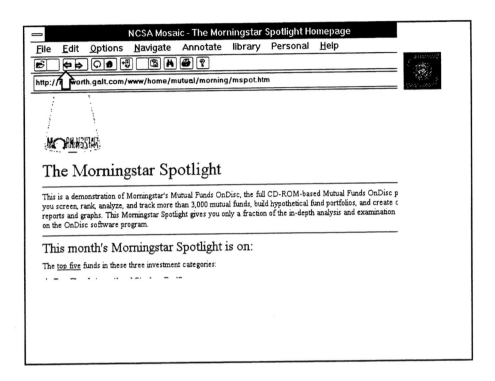

Morningstar is using its homepage as an advertisement for its services. It also gives free information on the top performers in three investment categories.

Before you can use this free information, you must become a registered user. Of course, once you have given your name and address, you have probably added your name to both electronic and paper mailing lists for their product.

Now take some time to navigate up several menu screens to view some other business information options.

Click on the left arrow icon button until you reach the Yahoo index "Economy: Markets and Investments: Mutual Funds."

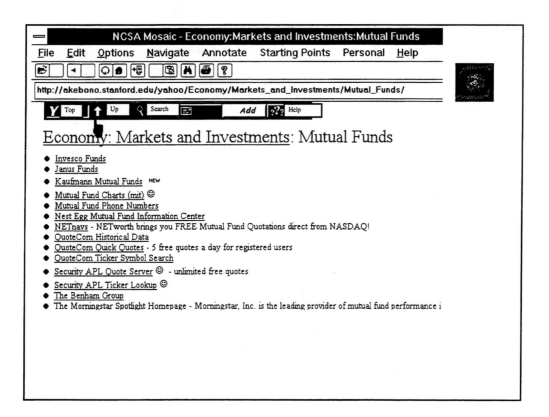

To go up one more menu level, click on the "up arrow" button.

Now click on the "corporations" submenu.

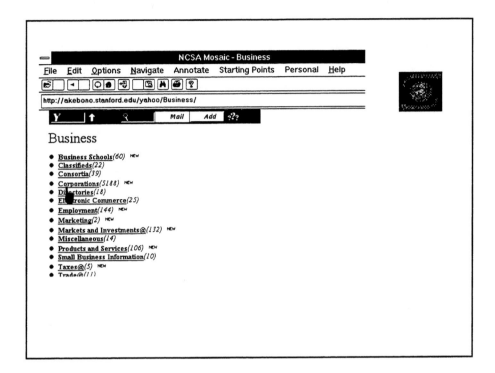

Then select the entry for Bank of America to see what type of information that corporation has on the Internet.

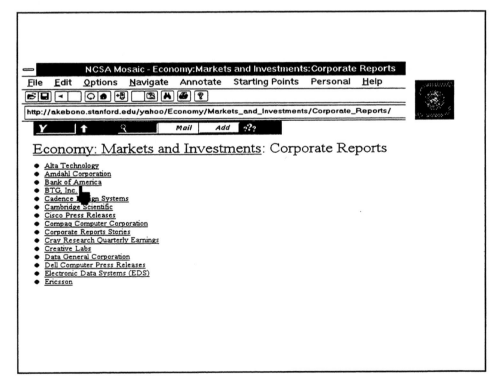

The Bank of America homepage serves as an index to recent news releases from the company's communications office. By clicking on any of the underlined (or highlighted) words, you have access to the full text of the release.

Click on the left arrow icon to return to the Yahoo index.

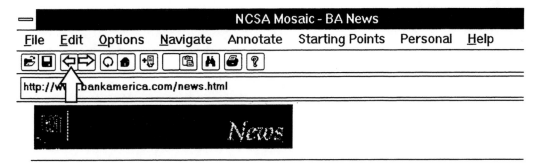

News

BankAmerica Announcements

BankAmerica Corporation is a diversified, global financial services company with customers across the United St around the world. In 1994, public announcements distributed by the company's corporate communications group i

- BankAmerica Corporation Wins Fed Approval for Expanded Activities in Section 20 Subsidiary (October 11,
- California's Largest Bank and Largest Grocery Retailer To Form New Alliance (September 29, 1994)
- BankAmerica Corporation, Arbor National Holdings, Inc., Announce Definitive Merger Agreement (Septemb
- President Clinton Announces New $50 Million Community Development Goal by Bank of America (Septemb
- BankAmerica Celebrates Completion of Continental Acquisition, Announces New Management Teams (Sept 1994)
- BankAmerica, Continental Bank Corporation Complete Merger Transaction (September 1, 1994)
- BofA Arbitration a Victory for Consumers (August 18, 1994)

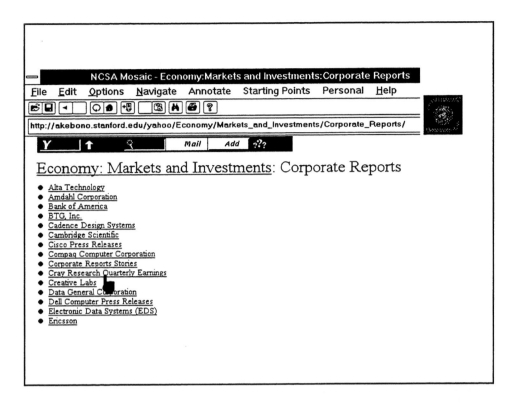

To explore the Cray Research Quarterly Earnings reports, click on that entry.

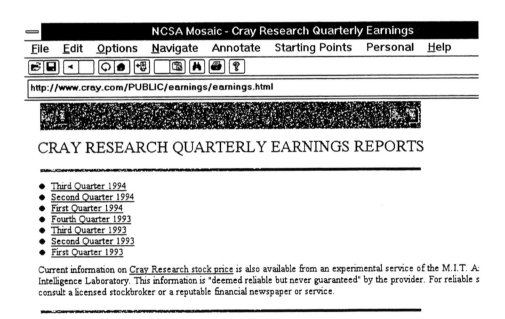

The Cray Research homepage provides earnings information for a number of different quarters. View Cray stock price information available at MIT by clicking on the underlined or highlighted text.

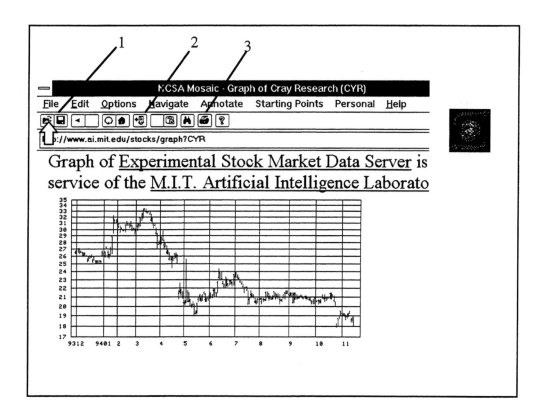

When you look at the graph provided at this site, suppose it contains information you want to save or print. To save the information to disk, click on the floppy icon (1) or click on the File pulldown menu and select Save." To print out the graph, click on the printer icon (3) or click on the File pulldown menu and select Print.

If you want to save this address in a hotlist—your personal directory of Internet addresses that will allow you to quickly return to this site without having to rekey the sequences of long URLs—you can either click on the add-to-hotlist icon (2) or select the Navigate pulldown menu and select "Add to current hotlist."

   Note: Instead of "hotlist" some systems use the term *bookmark*, a metaphor which conveys its function as a placeholder.

You can use previously-saved addresses in your hotlist file to go directly to other business sites by clicking on the opened-file icon, which you do to open a directory box.

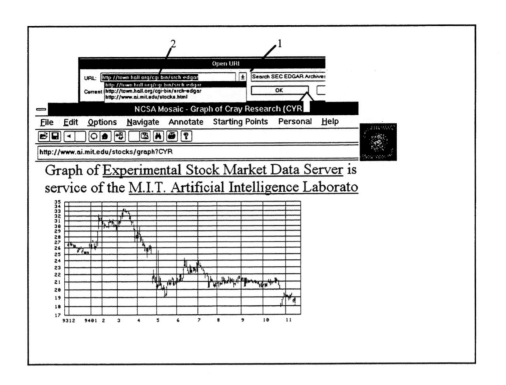

When the Open URL box appears, click on the down arrow (1). You are presented with several addresses that were on your hotlist. Click on the URL http://town.hall.org/cgi-bin/srch-edgar (2), then on the "OK" button. You are connected to the EDGAR database.

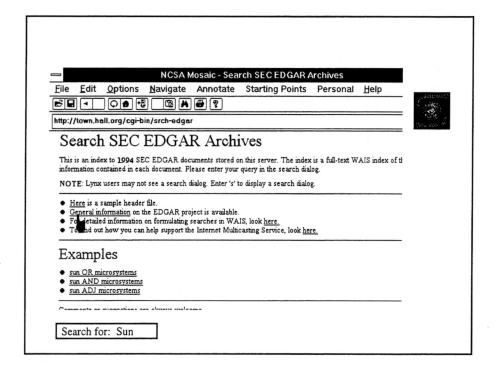

The SEC EDGAR Archives contains the full text of 10-K reports that were electronically filed after 1993. This site contains free information and, unlike the commercial sites we viewed earlier, does not require registration or payments. "Search SEC EDGAR Archives" allows you to search the database by company name and then display the text of these long annual reports. If, for instance, you wanted to locate the report for Sun Microsystems, just type the word *Sun* in the "Search for" box.

Note that there are help and information options at the top of the screen that explain such topics as how to perform searches and general information on the EDGAR project. This site provides good instructions on how to do sophisticated searches.

Click on "General Information" to get a description of the archive.

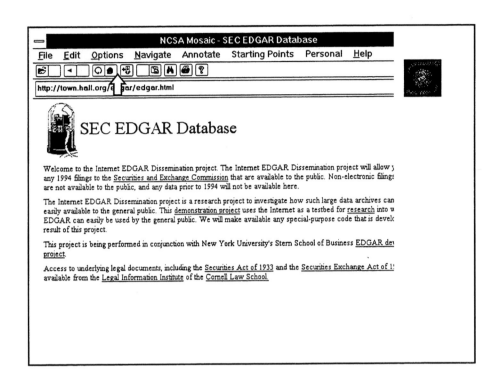

The EDGAR homepage gives an overview of the program and, as with the other locations that you have viewed, contains marked-up text or links that can connect you to other information sources on topics such as the Securities and Exchange Commission, the nature of the EDGAR demonstration project, and various law-related sites.

When you are through exploring this site, you can return to your homepage by clicking on the home icon button.

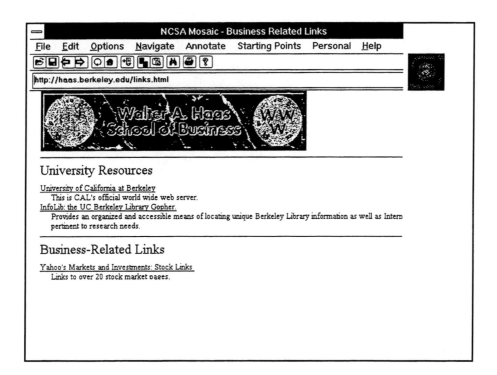

TIPS FOR CUSTOMIZING YOUR WEB BROWSER FOR SPEED OR EASE

Web browsers such as Mosaic and Netscape can be customized to allow you to obtain information more quickly, more elaborately, or with larger amounts of information showing on your screen.

Speeding up

Often you may not want to wait for large graphics files to be transferred and loaded by your computer. To tyrn off the automatic loading of images that slow down the information transfer process in

Mosaic   1. Click on the Options pull-down menu.

           2. Click on preferences.

           3. Click on the boxes in the Inline Images section so that the Dislplay Inline Images option does not have an "X" in it.

Netscape 1. Click on the Options pul-down menue.

           2. Click on the Auto Load Images option so the check mark disappears.

Seeing More Information

At other times, you may want to see more information on your screen. The buttons and icons that appear on your screen provide you with convenient means of navigating and editing, but they also limit the size of your screen used for showing the information that you are importing. To reduce the icons and menus and increase the viewing screen in:

Mosaic   1. Click on Options.

                   2. Click on the Show Toolbar, Show Status Bar, or Show Current URL, and remove the check marks next to these options to remove these features.

                   3. Or click on the Presentation Mode selection to remove Mosaic information and fill the entire screen with information from your remote login. To return to your Mosaic screen, hit the **Escape** key.

Netscape   1. Click on Options.

                   2. Click on the Show Toolbar, Show Directory button, or Show Location and remove the check marks next to these options to remove these features.

Review

In this demonstration, you have electronically traveled from coast to coast with some stops in between merely by clicking on marked text or icons on the screen. You have seen how a hierarchical subject index such as Yahoo can connect you to thousands of locations that have business information. You have witnessed how a graphical program such as Mosaic can search the Internet, save or print information, and create hotlists so you can return directly to sites you like. You have had a glimpse at how companies are using the Internet to advertise their products and sell their resources directly on the Net.

Now turn to "Best Bets for Exploration" (page 3) or use an online index such as Yahoo to find on your own many other business sources on the Net.

INDEX

10-K reports in *EDGAR Archives* 129

Academic Listservs 4

Academic Position Network 16

Access to the Internet, how to get 33

Accounting, discussion group on teaching
    (CTI-ACC-BUSINESS) 6

Accounting, Internet resources on 6-7

Accounting network, international (*ANET*) 6

Address (definition) 18

Addresses
    description of 35
    how to find 43
    how to read email 42

AJBS-L (discussion group) 12

ANET, International accounting network 6

anonymous FTP
    definition 18
    how to use 69

Archie
    definition 18
    use to find information (exercise) 79-81

Association of Japanese Business Studies,
    discussion group (AJBS-L) 12

Auditing, discussion group on 6

Babson College (Gopher site) 4

Bank of America homepage (in exercise) 124-125

Banking and consumer information (FDIC) 8

Banking and finance, index to working papers on
    (*NBER Working Papers*) 11

Banking, commercial and investment, discussion
    group (*Financial Economics Network*) 10

Banking statistics (*Federal Deposit Insurance
    Corporation*) 10

Banking statistics (*Federal Reserve Board Data*) 10

Basic Guide to Exporting 12

Best Bets for Exploration 3-17

Bibliography 22

Big Dreams (Web newsletter) 8

Bills and laws, federal (*Marvel*) 14

Binary form, transferring files in 71

Bookmark
    commands in Gopher 97, 107
    definition 18
    in Gopher, making a 96-97, 107

Bookmark *continued*
    in Mosaic, adding (exercise) 127
    in Mosaic, icon for adding 113

Business information via the Library of Congress
    (exercise) 51-57

Business-related discussion group, join a (exercise) 46

Business Resource Center 8

Business resources on the Internet, general 4-6

Business resources, Yahoo menu 117

Business use of the Internet 32

BUSLIB-L (discussion group) 4

California legislation, text of bills and Code 13

California State Senate Legislative Database 13

Canadian tax information, forms, codes
    (*Taxing Times*) 12

Catalog of Federal Domestic Assistance
    (via *Marvel*) 14

CICA Windows Archive 4

Client (definition) 18

Clinton, Bill (President) and Al Gore, role in
    Internet development 30

CNI Management 15

Commands
    FTP commands 20, 70-71
    Gopher commands 20-21, 87
    quick guide to 20-21
    Telnet commands 20, 50

Commercenet 5

Commercial services, examples of 119-120, 121-122

Commercial Services on the Net, Web site 5

Commercial use of the Internet 32

Commodities information (*Quotecom Data Service*) 12

Commodities reports (*Holt's*) 11

Companies, information about (*Hoover's Online*) 11

Computational Economics, Sara 16

Conferences on management (upcoming),
    announcements of (*Management Archive*) 15

Congress (103rd and 104th), bills, resolutions, and
    statutes of (*Thomas*) 14

Consumer information (FDIC) 8

Consumer Price Index using Veronica, searching for
    (exercise) 101-107

Consumer Product Safety Commission information
    (via *Marvel*) 14

Copying and pasting material in Mosaic, icon for 113

Corporate reports, Yahoo menu (in exercise) 124

CORRYFEE (discussion group) 7

Cost of living in U.S. cities, relative (*Relocation Salary Calculator*) 8

Country Reports on Economic Policy and Trade Practices 12

Cray Research Quarterly Earnings homepage (in exercise) 126

Cray Research stock price information (in exercise) 126-128

CTI-ACC-AUDIT (discussion group) 6

CTI-ACC-BUSINESS (discussion group) 6

Defenselink 13

Demographic information for marketing (*Upclose*) 16

DIMACS (*Discrete Mathematics and Theoretical Computer Science*) 16

Discrete Mathematics and Theoretical Computer Science 16

Discussion group, join a business-related (exercise) 46

Discussion groups, selected business-related

    AJBS-L 12

    BUSLIB-L 4

    CORRYFEE 7

    CTI-ACC-BUSINESS 6

    CTI-ACC-AUDIT 6

    ESBDC-L 9, 15

    Elmar 15

    FEDTAX-L 7

    Financial Economics Network 10

    GLOBMKT 15

    HRD-L 17

    NEWPROD 9, 16

Discussion groups, types of 44

Domains, email 42

Dow Jones publications, articles from (*Money & Investing Update from the Wall Street Journal*) 11

ECONDATA 7, 9

Economic Bulletin Board 7

Economic data, national and regional (*ECONDATA*) 7

Economic issues, discussion group on (CORRYFEE) 7

Economic information, by country (NTDB) 8

Economic information, Internet resources on 7-8

Economic Policy and Trade Practices, Country Reports on 12

Economic Working Papers 7

Economy: Markets and Investments, Yahoo menus 115, 117-119

Economy, statistical information on (*Economic Bulletin Board*) 7

EDGAR, EDGAR82 7, 10

EDGAR CIK AND TICKER LOOKUP 10

EDGAR using Mosaic, exercise in accessing 128-130

Egopher (*Entrepreneurship Gopher*) 8

Elmar (discussion group) 15

Email

    as an Internet function 34, 41

    use to join a discussion group (exercise) 46

    workshop module on 41-46

Email addresses

    how to find 43

    how to read 42

Email Quoter 10

Emailing a remote file to yourself using Gopher 98-99, 106

Entrepreneurs in biotech, Web site for 8

Entrepreneurs on the Web 9

Entrepreneur's Reference Guide, accessing full text of 51-57, esp. 56-57

Entrepreneurship Gopher 8

Entrepreneurship, Internet resources on 8-9

ESBDC-L (discussion group) 9, 15

Exercises

    join a business discussion group 46

    pre-workshop exercise 4-17

    Telnet to Washburn Law Library 58-64

    Telnet to Library of Congress 51-57

    use Archie to find information by subject 79-81

    use FTP to retrieve software 72-78

    use Gopher to find business statistics 88-99

    use Veronica to search for CPI 101-107

    use Mosaic and Yahoo on WWW to find business-related resources 113-130

Exporters, trade information for (*International Business Practices*) 12

Exporting American products (*Basic Guide to Exporting*) 12

FDIC Directory 8

Federal bills and laws, full text of (*Thomas*) 13

Federal Deposit Insurance Corporation 10

Federal Depository Insurance Corporation Directory 8

Federal Reserve Board Data 10

Federal tax information, forms, etc. (*Taxing Times*) 12

Federal taxation, discussion group on (FEDTAX-L) 7

FEDTAX-L (discussion group) 7

FedWorld Information Network 13

File Transfer Protocol *see FTP*

Finance and investment, Internet resources on 9-12

Finance, discussion group on teaching (CTI-ACC-BUSINESS) 6

Finance, index to working papers on (*NBER Working Papers*) 11

Finance, working papers series on (IBER) 11

Finance-related working papers (*NetEc*) 11

Financial data (*ECONDATA*) 9

Financial economics, discussion group (Financial Economics Network) 10

Financial Economics Network (discussion group) 10

Finding business-related statistics using Gopher (exercise) 88-99

Finding Consumer Price Index using Veronica (exercise) 101-107

Finding email addresses 43

Finding information on a subject using Archie (exercise) 79-81

Finger command 43

FINWEB 11

Food and Drug Administration, information from (via *Marvel*) 14

Foreign business and international trade, Internet resources on 12-13

Frustrations using the Internet 37-38

FTP

  as an Internet function 34

  basic facts about 69

  commands 19, 70-71

  definition 18

  use to retrieve Mosaic software (exercise) 72-78

  use to retrieve information about NAFTA (exercise) 79-81

  workshop module on 67-81

Functions, Internet 34

Gallup Poll results 15

The Gate 5

GLOBMKT (discussion group) 15

Glossary 17-18

Goods and services (*Entrepreneurs on the Web*) 9

Gopher

  basic facts about 86

  bookmark commands 97

  commands 19-20, 87

  definition 18

  use to find Consumer Price Index (exercise) 101-107

  use to find statistical information (exercise) 88-99

  workshop module on 83-107

Gopher Jewels 5

Gopherspace, using Veronica to search (exercise) 101-107, esp. 103

Gore, Al (Vice-president), role in Internet development of 30

Government information, gateway to (*Marvel*) 13

Government-produced information, Internet resources for obtaining 13

Government publications and legal resources on the Internet 13-14

Grant information, gateway to finding government (*Marvel*) 14

Graphics displays in Mosaic, how to turn off 112

Help in Mosaic, icon for getting 113

Holt's Stock Market Reports 11

Homepage 113, 114

Hoover's Online 11

Host (definition) 18

Hotlist in Mosaic

  adding to (exercise) 127

  icon for adding to 113

HRD-L (discussion group) 17

HTML (definition) 18

Human Resources, Internet resources on 17

Hypermedia documents 110

Inktomi Search Engine 5

Institute of Business and Economic Research 11

Internal Revenue Service Homepage 10

International Accounting Network 6

International Business Practices 12

International trade, Internet resources on 12-13
Internet
    basic information about 29
    definition 18
    development of 29, 30
Internet Sources of Government Information 13
Investment, Internet resources on 9-12
IRS Homepage 11

Japan Information (Gopher site) 13
Japanese business studies, discussion
    group (AJBS-L) 12
Job announcements in higher education (Academic
    Position Network) 17
Job openings and job seekers' resumes (Online Career
    Center) 17
Join a business discussion group (exercise) 46
Journals, selected business-related
    Big Dreams 8

Labor data (Time Series Data) 8
Law-related business sources 14
Law resources, accessing (exercise) 58-64
Legal and business information, accessing
    (exercise) 58-64
Legal Information Institute 14
Legal information sources (Washington and Lee Law
    Library System) 14
Legal resources on the Internet 13-14
Legislative history, federal (Marvel) 14
Library of Congress, Telnet to business information
    via (exercise) 51-57
Library of Congress's Marvel 13
List managers 44
List of Marketing Lists (Mousetracks) 16
Listprocessor, a discussion list manager 44
Listserv, a discussion list manager 44
Listserv, how to join 45
Listserv/listserver (definition) 18
login (definition) 18
Long Business & Economics Library 5

Mail servers as a discussion group form 44
Mailing a remote file to your email address using
    Gopher 98-99, 106
Majordomo, a discussion list manager 44

Management Archive 15
Management, Internet resources on 15
Management of small business, discussion group
    (ESBDC-L) 15
Management, working papers on (Gopher site) 7
Managers, training of (CNI Management) 15
Market data (Quotecom Data Service) 12
Marketing
    addresses on the Internet (Mousetracks) 16
    advice on (Marketing to Consumers) 16
    demographic information (Upclose) 16
    discussion group on (GLOBMKT) 15
    Internet resources on 15-16
Marketing research, discussion group on (Elmar) 15
Marketing to Consumers, an Outline 16
Markets and investments, Yahoo menus 115, 117-119
Marvel (Library of Congress)
    description of site and access information 14
    Telnet to business resources via (exercise) 51-57
Mathematics and computer science (Discrete
    Mathematics) 16
Money & Investing Update from the Wall Street
    Journal 11
Morningstar Spotlight (example of commercial
    service) 121-122
Mosaic
    basic facts about 110-112
    definition 18
    developments 111
    problems using 112
    software, retrieving and downloading
        (exercise) 72-78
    tips 131-132
    use to find business resources (exercise) 110-131
    use to find information about mutual funds
        (exercise) 113-122
Mousetracks (Web site) 16
Mutual funds, exercise in finding information
    about 113-122

NAFTA, search for information about (exercise) 80-81
National economic data (ECONDATA) 7
National Technical Information Service (FedWorld) 13
National Trade Data Bank 8
NBER Working Papers 11
Net (definition) 18

Netcruiser 110
NetEc 11
Netfind 43
Netscape 110, 131, 132
Netsurf 5
Network (definition) 18
Networks, number of 31
New product development process, discussion group on (NEWPROD) 9
NEWPROD (discussion group) 9, 16
Newsgroups as a discussion group form 44
NTIS FedWorld (*FedWorld*) 13

Online Career Center 17
Operations and statistical methods, Internet resources on 16
Overview of workshop 24-25

PAWWS Financial Network 12
Personnel, Internet resources on 17
President's press release, accessing text of (exercise) 58-64
Pre-workshop exercise 4-16
Printing in Mosaic, icon for 113
Printing information using Mosaic (exercise) 127
Programming codes, mathematical (*Bilkent*) 15
Protocol (definition) 18

Quality 15
Quotecom Data Service 12
QuoteCom Historical Data (example of commercial service) 119-120

Regional economic data (Gopher site) 7
Regulations, federal (*Marvel*) 14
Reloading screens in Mosaic, icon for 113
Relocation Salary Calculator 8
RiceInfo 6

San Francisco *Chronicle* and *Examiner* 5
Saving information using Mosaic (exercise) 127
Saving to disk in Mosaic, icon for 113
Searching for a term in Mosaic, icon for 113
Searching Gophers using Veronica 101-107
SEC EDGAR (in exercise) 128-130
Securities and Exchange Commission, filings to (*EDGAR, EDGAR CIK*) 7, 10

Server (definition) 18
Small Business Administration, information from (via *Marvel*) 14
Small Business Advancement National Center 9
Small Business Development Centers, discussion group on (ESBDC-L) 9
Small businesses, Web newsletter for (*Big Dreams*) 8
Small businesses, Web site for providing help to (*Business Resource Center*) 8

Software, retrieving (exercise) 72-78
Speed access in Mosaic, how to 112
State tax information, forms, codes (*Taxing Times*) 12
Statistical information, finding using Gopher (exercise) 88-99
Statistical information on the U.S. economy (*Economic Bulletin Board*) 7
Statistical methods, Internet resources on 16
Statistical programs, gateway to (*Statlib*) 16
Statlib 16
Stock market reports (*Holt's*) 11
Stock prices, daily (*Email Quoter*) 10
Stock-related information (*Email Quoter*) 10
Stocks information (*Quotecom Data Service*) 12
Subject access using Archie (exercise) 79-81
Subscribe to a business discussion group (exercise) 46
Subscribing to a listserv 45
Sun Microsystems' annual report using EDGAR, example of accessing 129
Survey of Current Business, data tables from 9

Tax forms and information 11, 12
Taxation discussion group, federal (FEDTAX-L) 7
Taxing Times 12
TCP/IP 19, 29
Teaching accounting, discussion group on (CTI-ACC-BUSINESS) 6
Telnet
    as an Internet function 34
    basic facts about 49
    commands 19, 50
    definition 19
    use to find business and legal information (exercises) 51-64
    workshop module on 47-65
10-K reports in *EDGAR Archives* 129
The Gate 5

Theoretical computer science (*Discrete Mathematics*) 16

Thomas (via Library of Congress) 14

Time Series Data 8

TQM in manufacturing and service industries (*Quality*) 15

Trade information for exporters (*International Business Practices*) 12

Trade Practices, Country Reports on Economic Policy and 12

Trends in Internet development 30

U.S. Bureau of Labor Statistics (*Time Series Data*) 7

U.S. Department of Defense, information from (*Defenselink*) 13

U.S. economy, statistical information on (Gopher site) 7

Uniform Resource Locators 36

Upclose Demographic Summaries 16

URL file in Mosaic, icon for opening 113

URLs 36

Usenet News as a discussion group form 44

Uses of the Internet by businesses 32

Veronica
    basic facts about 100
    definition 19
    use to search for Consumer Price Index (exercise) 101-107

W3 *see World Wide Web*

Wall Street Journal (*Money & Investing Update from the Wall Street Journal*) 11

Washburn Law Library, Telnet to (exercise) 58-64

Washington and Lee Law Library System 14

Web *see World Wide Web*

Whitehouse Homepage 14

Working papers on economics and management (Gopher site) 7

Working papers on finance-related information (*NetEc*) 11

Working papers series on finance, citations to (IBER) 11

Workshop overview 24-25

World Wide Web
    basic facts about 110
    definition 19
    tips 131-132
    workshop module on 109-131

WWW *see World Wide Web*

Yahoo
    main menu 116
    use to find business information (exercise) 114-119
    Web gateway to business resources 6